Twayne's English Authors Series

EDITOR OF THIS VOLUME

Arthur F. Kinney
University of Massachusetts, Amherst

James Shirley

TEAS 321

JAMES SHIRLEY

By BEN LUCOW

St. John's University

TWAYNE PUBLISHERS

A DIVISION OF G. K. HALL & CO., BOSTON

Copyright © 1981 by G. K. Hall & Co.

Published in 1981 by Twayne Publishers,
A Division of G. K. Hall & Co.
All Rights Reserved

Printed on permanent/durable acid-free paper and bound
in the United States of America

First Printing

Library of Congress Cataloging in Publication Data

Lucow, Ben.
James Shirley.

(Twayne's English authors series; TEAS 321)
Bibliography: p. 165–72
Includes index.
1. Shirley, James, 1596–1666—Criticism and interpretation.
PR3147.L8   822'.4   80–29503
ISBN 0–8057–6716–9

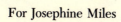

For Josephine Miles

Contents

About the Author

Since 1965 Ben Lucow has taught Renaissance and modern drama at St. John's University, New York, where he is Associate Professor of English. He earned a Ph.D. in English at the University of Washington and presented excerpts from his study of John Ford at a NWMLA conference. For the University of California he participated in the Far East Command Program and in the administration of the University-wide Student Writing Program. His publications include critical studies for journals such as *Notes on Modern American Literature* and *Studies in Short Fiction*. He has acted in or directed dramas by numerous playwrights from Shakespeare to Arthur Miller.

Preface

James Shirley's life and canon present no special problem for the critical biographer of an English Renaissance dramatist. Biographical data are minimal; bibliographical problems are inevitable. Shirley's life and work are thus no more or less accessible than those of most of his contemporaries and predecessors. The few documents unearthed (mainly by Albert C. Baugh and, more recently, Georges Bas) since the publication of Arthur H. Nason's 1915 study tend to substantiate the data in the main source of information about Shirley's life, Anthony à Wood's brief notes in *Athenae Oxonienses*, except for attendance at Oxford (which would qualify Shirley for inclusion in a book about its graduates) and conversion to Catholicism. Similarly, questions familiar to Shirley scholars—about his association with Gray's Inn, for example, or about the extent of his revisions of George Chapman's *Chabot*—remain open. However, conjectures about Shirley's life are less important in this study than the plays themselves, especially those whose authorship is unquestioned and whose dates of composition are well established.

After a biographical introduction and a chapter on masques and nondramatic verse, this study of Shirley's plays proceeds for the most part chronologically, not to trace development, for no significant change in style marks any stage of his career, but to relate the quality of his writing to the conditions under which he wrote. Discussion of individual works in Chapters 2 to 8 includes plot summary, relevant background information, and critical analysis. Although each play is dealt with both on its own merits and as a part of Shirley's total achievement, the emphasis is on analysis of individual plays. The last chapter sums up Shirley's uniqueness and his place in the history of English dramatic literature.

To approach Shirley as workmanlike playwright for the Caroline stage is to acknowledge the influence on his writing of contemporary tastes, of which he sometimes complained. Shirley aspired to literary excellence, but as dramatist for acting companies he gave primary attention to their need for steady patronage. Spectacle, intricate plotting, and witty dialogue apparently drew the largest London audiences of the 1620s and 1630s. The greatest English dramatists, writing under similar conditions, often contributed impressively to literature, but Shirley only infrequently. Much that is fine in his work appears alongside much that is pedestrian and indifferent. In only a few of his thirty-odd extant plays does he produce a superior blend of his theatrical stock.

Critical editions of individual plays (many still-unpublished doctoral dissertations) have appeared with increasing frequency since the 1930s, suggesting a greater current interest in Shirley than at any other time since the seventeenth century. That interest is largely academic, however, for productions of even the anthologists' favorites *(The Lady of Pleasure, Hyde Park, The Cardinal)* are rare in the twentieth. In the absence of a definitive critical edition of Shirley's collected works, quotations in this study are from the earliest editions, available on microfilm, with scene divisions according to modern editions. The original spelling and punctuation have been retained, except that i-j and u-v have been regularized. Emendation, indicated by square brackets, is limited to obvious misprints: "Subjects, methin[k]s, are crown'd as we[ll] as kings" for "Subjects, methings, are crown'd as we as kings."

I am grateful to the staffs of the Columbia University Butler Library, the New York Public Library, the Queens College Library, and the St. John's University Library for their help in locating copies of the earliest editions of Shirley's works; to Ferdinand Bachman of St. John's University for commentary on the original draft of this study; to James Hafley of St. John's University for criticism and encouragement at every stage of the project; and to Arthur Kinney of the University of Massachusetts for a thorough editorial review.

BEN LUCOW

St. John's University

Chronology

	Royal Master; The Doubtful Heir; St. Patrick for Ireland; The Gentleman of Venice; The Politician; (?) revision of George Chapman's *Chabot*.
1640	Return (April) to England.
1640– 1642	Dramatist for King Charles's company; *The Imposture*.
1641	*The Cardinal*.
1642	*The Sisters; The Court Secret;* theaters closed.
1646	*Poems &c. by James Shirley*.
1646– 1666	Teacher, Whitefriars.
1649	*Via ad Latinam Linguam Complanata*.
1653	*Cupid and Death*.
1656	*The Rudiments of Grammar*.
1658	*Honoria and Mammon; The Contention of Ajax and Ulysses*.
1660	*Manductio*.
1666	Dies; buried October 29, St. Giles in the Fields, London.

CHAPTER 1

"First Fruits":
The Life of James Shirley:
1596–1666

THEATER in London was flourishing in 1596, the year of James Shirley's birth. Shakespeare had already made enough money acting in and writing plays to purchase New Place; at twenty-four, Ben Jonson was beginning as an actor. Most of the greatest English Renaissance plays appeared during the next two decades, when Shirley was growing up. Like Jonson a Londoner born and bred, Shirley was twenty-nine when he emerged as a playwright in 1625, the first year of Charles I's reign. After Jonson's break with Inigo Jones in 1631, the influential architect-designer won for Shirley the opportunity to write an elaborate, highly successful masque for the court, *The Triumph of Peace*, produced in 1633. Shirley worked assiduously for seventeen years to accommodate the tastes of his largely aristocratic audiences. Successor to two generations that had produced at least half a dozen master dramatists, Shirley dominated the English stage until the theaters closed in 1642. After the Restoration some of his plays of the years 1625–42 were produced successfully, but Shirley wrote no new ones in the 1660s. Within a few years of his death in 1666, the new generation of playwrights, probably most influenced by John Dryden, were denigrating Shirley's work. His literary reputation since then has improved somewhat, but it has never regained the peak it reached in the 1630s.

Prolific and competent at his craft, Shirley maintained a respectable level of literary achievement for one so thoroughly conditioned by the peculiar demands of his time and place. He wrote for a theater that exploited a sensationalism of the Elizabethan and Jacobean variety without attendant intellectual challenge: the obligatory

philosophizing and moralizing of Caroline drama in general stands
in pale contrast to the colorful, often profound dramatic utterance
of the earlier periods. Shirley only occasionally penetrated beyond
contemporary theatrical limitations: a few of his plays surprise either
in their overall quite remarkable conception and execution or in
individual passages of charming lyricism.

An examination of his work and of what little is known of his life
yields an image of a conventionally moral Christian gentleman, a
well-educated middle-class family man who nevertheless delighted
in the spectacle of high fashion in the city and at court. His taste
for pageantry and ritual helps explain both his passionate allegiance
to the Royalist cause and persistent rumors of his conversion to
Roman Catholicism. Shirley was inclined by temperament (if not
necessarily by reason of birth, social position, or education) toward
the dominant Cavalier sensibility of the late 1620s and 1630s.

I *Gentleman and Scholar*

According to Anthony à Wood, Shirley was the descendant of a
prominent Sussex or Warwickshire family.[1] Another seventeenth-
century antiquarian, Thomas Dingley, describes Shirley's coat of
arms: "SHIRLEY, James, a famous Poet, my schoolmaster, bore
paly of 6 Or and azure a Canton erminee."[2] But Shirley's ancestry
remains a matter of speculation.[3] Arthur H. Nason in his biographical
and critical study of James Shirley considers at some length three
possible family trees and suggests a fourth, but wisely avoids naming
any as definitely Shirley's.[4] Perhaps because he really believed he
was descended from a noble family, Shirley nurtured his taste for
the manners of English aristocracy. His affinity for the court circle
of Charles and Henrietta Maria may account in part for the ideali-
zation of romantic love among the courtier characters in his plays.

Whatever his ancestry, Shirley was born in 1596 to a family that
provided him with more than adequate schooling. He began his
formal education in 1608 at the Merchant Taylors' school, which
offered a fairly rigorous classical curriculum of Latin, Greek, grammar, rhetoric, and logic. The school day began and ended with
devotional exercises and tests of the students' knowledge of the
Bible. Although Shirley's plays in comparison with those of earlier
English dramatists contain minimal classical and biblical allusion,
he must have been a good student, or at least a trustworthy one,

for the only record of his accomplishments at the school is his appointment as a monitor in 1612, his last year there.

From 1612 to 1615 Shirley may have worked exclusively as an apprentice to a scrivener or simultaneously studied briefly at St. John's College, Oxford, although no record exists of his attendance there. The young man's alleged facial disfigurement would disqualify him for the ministry, according to the Master of St. John's at the time, Doctor (later Archbishop) Laud, who nevertheless favored Shirley.[5] Whatever the course of Shirley's education for three years after leaving the Merchant Taylors' school, he was enrolled in 1615 at St. Catherine's College, Cambridge, where he received the Bachelor of Arts degree in 1617. Information about the next eight years is slight, but these data appear to be accurate: Shirley was ordained in 1617; he worked toward a higher degree at Cambridge from 1617 to 1620; he married Elizabeth Gilmet in 1618; he accepted a living in Wheathampstead, Lincolnshire, not too far from St. Albans, where a son was baptized in 1619. In 1620 he vacated the living for a teaching position at a grammar school in St. Albans. He left the school within five years to write for the stage in London. The impulse toward a literary career can be traced to the publication of a narrative poem in 1618, but nothing in the meager data available about Shirley before the production of *Love Tricks* in 1625 suggests any inclination toward the stage. Neither Wood nor any subsequent biographer of Shirley has ventured to explain the transition from teacher to playwright and the removal from St. Albans to Gray's Inn.

During his last five years in St. Albans Shirley may have converted to Catholicism.[6] The earliest direct reference, in Wood's *Athenae Oxonienses,* comes after Shirley's death. Documentation is lacking with "evidence . . . hard to come by, since in the England of Shirley's day Roman Catholicism was proscribed by the State and Catholics were often averse to acknowledging their religion publicly."[7] Scholars since Wood have either accepted his statement outright or supported it with inferences from cryptic allusions by Shirley's contemporaries in his lifetime and from the tenor of Shirley's own writings.[8]

Whether or not Shirley converted to Catholicism, he was clearly devoted to England's Queen Henrietta Maria, who was of French Catholic descent. Her marriage to Charles in 1625 undoubtedly meant that there would.be some relaxation of laws against English Catholics. Endymion Porter, a dilettante in drama compared to Shirley, and the son of a Spanish Catholic mother, exercised con-

siderable influence at court. Shirley enjoyed the queen's favor for
much of his career in the theater, although not enough, apparently,
to win him the poet-laureateship when Jonson died in 1637. Shirley
remained devoted to the court throughout his career as a playwright
and loyal to the Royalist cause when that career was over. The
conversion to Catholicism is supposed to have occurred in the early
1620s, before he began writing for the theater and before Charles
and Henrietta Maria came to the throne. The conversion would thus
appear to be a matter of personal conviction with no bearing on his
political beliefs or on his goals in the theater.

It would be interesting to know just how close was Shirley's association with Archbishop Laud during the reign of Charles I. Laud
founded and led the Anglican High Church movement, representing
only a minority of the English population, mostly those members
of the aristocracy and landed gentry who did not object either to
clerical authoritarianism or to the clergy's increased political power.
Laud's strictly enforced policies regarding religious worship in the
country's churches emphasized the importance of ritual instead of
the more popular preaching and thus alienated the majority of Englishmen, who otherwise might not have supported the Puritan cause.
Shirley's Royalist sympathies must have been engendered as much
by religious as political convictions, for, like most of the literary
Englishmen of his day (with Milton the major exception), he found
no fault in the Anglican variation of the Catholic Counter-Refor-
mation. If anything, the High Church movement did not go far
enough for Shirley, who shared the taste of many at court for Queen
Henrietta Maria's Catholicism.

After seventeen years as a dramatist Shirley served briefly (probably 1642–44) under Newcastle in the war against the Puritans. By
the mid-1640s he was back in London, where he joined a group of
scholars headed by Thomas Stanley.[9] After the war he taught in the
Whitefriars district of London. A grateful student's appreciation
suggests the quality of Shirley's teaching, according to John Gough
Nichols, who writes referring to Thomas Dingley,

We derive some intimation of Dingley's education from a passage at the
close of his first journal, where, having arrived at Calais on his return
homewards, he apologizes for the shortness of his account of that city by
the attractions of "the magnetic power of Dover cliffs," which, though scarce
discernible through a mist, drew his eyes thither, making good "this saying
often us'd by my worthy and learn'd schoolmaster, James Shirley, Poet-
laureat, PATRIAE FUMUS ALIENO IGNE LUCULENTIOR EST."[10]

Nichols also notes that with Dingley Shirley "was at least successful in implanting a lasting love of the classic poets, for our author's [Dingley's] journals are full of quotations from Virgil, Ovid, Horace, and others of the writers of antiquity, with occasional passages of Greek."[11]

The scholarly James Shirley published three grammar texts during the 1640s, 1650s and 1660s.[12] The subtitle of one of these, *The Rudiments of Grammar*, "The Rules Composed in English Verse, for the Greater Benefit and Delight of Young Beginners," describes a Latin and English grammar actually written mostly in prose, with some examples in couplets: "Verbs that are called Personal, must receive / Number and Person from their Nominative."[13] The last grammar text, *Manductio*, appeared in 1660, the year of the Restoration.

Shirley wrote nothing for the stage in the six remaining years of his life. In an address "To the Candid Reader" of *Honoria and Mammon*, published in 1659, Shirley says that this work "is now made public to satisfy the importunity of my friends: I will only add it is like to be the last, for in my resolve, nothing of this nature shall, after this, engage either my pen or invention." Although several of his plays written before 1642 were staged in the 1660s, Shirley held to his resolve. The Anglican priest manqué who took up teaching briefly before turning playwright withdrew permanently from the fashionable world of theater and royal court. He continued teaching in London until the Great Fire of 1666, when he and his wife removed to St. Giles in the Fields, Middlesex. There they died of old age and exhaustion, according to Wood, on the same day, October 29, 1666. The date is confirmed by an entry in the church register at St. Giles. Sixty years after Shirley's death appeared *An Essay towards an universal and rational grammar*, edited by Jenkin T. Philipps "from Shirley's grammatical writings."[14] Shirley's scholarly work may have been pedestrian, but it had greater currency after the Restoration period than his plays.

At least there is no doubt that Shirley was a scholar and a teacher for much of his adult life. The questions of conversion and ancestry remain open. It is not unlikely that Shirley converted to Catholicism, but there is no documentary evidence of conversion. And although it is unlikely that he was born to a noble family, he wrote and tried to live as if to the manner born.

II *Royalist and Romanticist*

Shirley's association with the court of King Charles I accounts for much in his work that smacks of special pleading: emphasis on a ruler's right to absolute power. Shirley's writings in whatever genre explicitly or implicitly extol the virtue of a divinely ordained social order headed by a king. He wholeheartedly supported Charles in all the king's struggles with Parliament in the 1630s and with the Puritan army in the 1640s.[15] He served under the Earl of Newcastle (Duke, after the Restoration), survived the war and the Interregnum, and must have rejoiced at the return from exile of the late king's heir in 1660. But Shirley's great days, like Charles I's, were over in 1642. Coincidentally, Shirley's seventeen years as leading playwright of the London theater exactly parallel those of Charles on the throne: his first play was produced the year Charles became king, and his last the year the king left London.

During those seventeen years, whether in or out of favor at court, Shirley consistently produced a species of drama designed to glorify kingship. Today the attribution of sanctity to a king's conduct of political affairs may seem excessive, but the same kind of sentiment appears in the writings of many Royalists. Early in Charles's reign Dr. Donne preached in the royal presence that "*God* hath commended our Spirits, not onely our civill peace, but our Religion, too, into the *hand* of the *Magistrate*."[16] The divine mission of a king could brook no higher earthly control: "But where there is an inducing of a *super-Soveraigne* . . . above our *Native and naturall Power* . . . this is a . . . destroying of . . . the *State*, the *Law*."[17] In 1642 Thomas Fuller described Charles as a mortal God (in *The Holy State and the Profane State*). The success of Charles's own *Eikon Basilike* ("royal image"; the "King's Book") came too late to save him from what many readers at the time considered his martyrdom. *Eikon Basilike*, one of the few genuine "best sellers" among twenty thousand publications dealing with mid-seventeenth-century political and religious controversies, had thirty-five printings in England alone within a year of its original publication in 1649, followed by several Continental translations into Latin, French, and other languages. Whether or not the pious meditations on the king's troubles during the 1640s are completely the work of Charles, the sentiments regarding royalty feature the same kind of exalted language linking divinity and kingship to be found elsewhere in works by English Royalists, including those by Shirley. His plays in this vein have a distinctive verbal texture that insists on the legitimacy of princely power, the value of hierarchy, and the opportunity for valorous conduct that life in a monarchy offers. The language of power, degree, and honor constitutes the basic terminology of Shirley's tragedies and tragicomedies in the evocation of an ideal princely court.

The image pattern unique to an individual play (the sea imagery in *The Court Secret* or the "cardinal" imagery in *The Cardinal*) is superimposed on a verbal structure common to all Shirley's dramas of court life. Within the first twenty lines of *The Cardinal* appear *counsel, advance, duchess, intelligence* (espionage), *governs, gallant gentleman, war, victory, courted, honour, praise, usurp, title, blood* (breeding), *noble ancestors, great family, king, helm of state,* and *privilege*. Such terms as *art* and *practice, darling, greatness, virtue, danger,* and *obey,* though less indigenous to a court setting, nevertheless further define the quality of life at court as one of intrigue, favoritism, and power politics, with honest men literally risking their lives when they challenge corrupt favorites or tyrannical princes. Shirley's language of court life bulwarks endorsement of a rigidly stratified society. Shirley the Royalist cherished his faith in the essential rightness of a monarchical state.[18]

A prince has a holy mission, which can be perverted by a schemer, often the prince's favorite. In *The Imposture* Flaviano, "the Dukes Creature," tells him why a prince may break a promise: "Princes are not / Oblig'd to keep, what their necessities / Contract, but prudently secure their states, /And dear posterity" (I.i). In a later scene he adds:

> Promise any thing
> In such a strait, and not despair to effect it.
> Be private men content with their poor Fathom,
> Since Heaven we limit not, why should not Kings,
> Next Gods, perform the second mighty things? (I.ii)

The heroine of the play, Juliana, reminds the Duke that he is honor bound to keep his promises: "You have a title yet more strong pleads for you, / The contract, and the promise of a Prince, / A chain with many Links of Adamant" (II.iii), for "Princely natures . . . are next to Forms Angelical" (V.iii). Kingship, religion, and nature are closely allied here, sharing the principle of universal order: "when /Princes

break faith, Religion must dissolve, / And nature grone with burthen
of the living" (I.i). In several plays Shirley thus examines in great
detail the moral-philosophical and religious bases of his concept of
kingship. The extent to which he allows his preoccupation to determine the course of action in plays with court settings suggests
an extra-artistic purpose. Plays like *The Imposture* seem to have
been designed as mediēval moralities were, to illustrate essentially
religious beliefs. And such plays could advance the king's cause in
the 1630s and early 1640s.

To advance the queen's cause, another kind of religion figures
rather prominently in Shirley's work: the "religion of love." A "Platonic Love" cult, a veritable religion of love, is said to have thrived
at the court of Charles and Henrietta Maria under the special aegis
of the queen:

> The Court affords little News at present, but that there is a Love call'd
> Platonick Love, which much sways there of late; it is a Love abstracted
> from all corporeal gross Impressions and sensual Appetite, but consists in
> Contemplations and Ideas of the Mind, not in any carnal Fruition. This
> Love sets the Wits of the Town on work; and they say there will be a Mask
> shortly of it, whereof Her majesty and her Maids of Honour will be part.[19]

"Her Majesty and her Maids of Honour" had already appeared in
a private production of Walter Montagu's *The Shepherd's Paradise*,
a pastoral play, in 1632. Among the "Wits of the Town on work"
none was more prolific than William Davenant, who wrote for the
"cult" *Love and Honour* (1634), *The Platonic Lovers* (a romantic
drama involving love potions and Platonic lovers versus fleshly ones)
(1635), and two masques: *The Temple of Love* (1635) and *The
Triumph of the Prince D'Amour* (1636).

The Platonic love cult probably had more communicants on stage
than at court. It was codified, according to George Sensabaugh, in
"court plays . . . written for the specific purpose of making clear
the philosophy of the cult."[20] Sensabaugh analyzes the code under
these headings: "fate rules all lovers"; "beauty and goodness are one
and the same"; "beautiful women are saints to be worshiped"; "true
love is of equal hearts and divine"; "love is all-important and all-
powerful"; "true love is the sole guide to virtue"; and "true love
allows any liberty of action and thought."[21] Much has been written
about the cult, but its importance can be overestimated. The royal
pair themselves clearly reserved their affection for each other in

good times and bad: after 1644, when Henrietta returned to France, never to see Charles again, they exchanged letters addressed respectively to "Mon Cher Coeur" and "Dear Heart" that record an enduring mutual respect and love.[22]

Perhaps the cult Henrietta Maria sponsored is most charitably viewed today as a harmless source of amusement for the golden boys and girls in the queen's entourage. None of the glamorous crew outshone the naturalized Flemish painter Anthony Van Dyck, whose portraits of Charles and Henrietta Maria helped create the romantic image of their court that persists into our own time. Some courtiers, such as the flamboyant Van Dyck, may have taken advantage of the ambience at Whitehall Palace, but the conduct of the court generally was more circumspect than that of James I. An occasional scandal did involve one or another of the queen's favorites. "Immorality was thought to 'be rife in the queen's circle, and the reputation of Her Majesty did not escape the implications of gossip. While without blemish herself, the queen was tolerant of the misdoings of others."[23] The love cult may have come about because of Henrietta Maria's desire to introduce a little Continental sophistication into the English court.

Henrietta Maria was a very young bride and queen, sixteen years old when she married Charles and came to the throne of England. At first her influence at court was slight: shortly after marriage Charles, at the urging of the Duke of Buckingham, his chief adviser on foreign affairs, ordered her retinue (including several Catholic priests), back to France. After Buckingham's assassination in 1628, Charles and Henrietta Maria became a loving couple who saw eye to eye on all matters concerning country and court. Both were patrons of the arts; both sponsored and maintained acting companies; it was Charles who persuaded Van Dyck to settle in England; and Charles had no objection to the queen's private theatricals.

Was the cult as innocent in its original intent as the queen's interest in the stage? It would seem that the cult's effect on the practice of Caroline dramatists was more significant than anything that went on at court. Shirley and his fellows drew their models, if not their inspiration, for their aristocratic characters from the ideal lovers Henrietta Maria's courtiers aspired to be. And the existence of the cult could help explain why Shirley has so much to say about love, ideal and not so ideal.

In *The Young Admiral* observations on love range widely from complaints about its effect on sanity to awesome testaments to its

holiness: "nothing can be / Too precious to forfeit" for love, exclaims
Cesario, "I am mad" (I.i). His beloved's absence "teares" his
"braine" (II.i). Vittori claims curative powers for Cassandra's kisses
and tears: "had *Vittori* taken / Into his body a thousand wounds,
this kisse / Had made me well againe, or but one droppe / Of this
rich balsome, for I know thy teares / Are joy to see *Vittori* safe"
(I.ii). The victorious young admiral considers her love "a greater
empire . . . Then fame or victorie hath ever boasted" (ibid.). Their
love, says Cassandra, is a mystical union more precious than life:
"we are one soule, life cannot be / So precious as our loves" (III.i).
But it is also a disease: "I am thy / Affliction," says Vittori (ibid.).
"The wounds" of love are deep, says Rosinda, and "Can find no cure
without his surgerie / That left them in my bosome" (IV.i). True
lovers are made for each other: Cassandra tells Cesario, "*Rosinda*
was by heaven / Design'd for you, as I was for Vittori" (V.iii). It
should be noted that no sense of extravagance, no hint of irony,
accompanies these utterances. Their intensity testifies to the inef-
fable power of ideal love.

   The Royal Master features the language of the "religion of love"
prominently. Montalto compares Domitilla to a saint (I.ii) and wor-
ships and sacrifices at her altar: "Ile creepe and kisse thy Altar Love"
(II.ii), "which must be / Made crimson with the blood of a true
lover" (III.i). Domitilla's beauty elicits extravagant praise from Octavio:

> those eyes
> Are able to create another *Indies;*
> All the delights that dwell in blessed *Tempe*
> Divinely bud and blossome in your cheeke;
> The treasure of *Arabia's* in your breath;
> Nor *Thebes* alone, as to *Amphions* Lute
> Stoopes to the heavenly magicke of your voyce,
> But all the world. (III.iii)

Domitilla wants "No more of this; these praises / Are made for children, and will make truth blush." She means that such praises
coming from Montalto are made for children; the same praises from
a true love are made in heaven. The Duke, who also loves Domitilla,
declares, "if she prove / Gentle, my heart I consecrate to love." In
the next act he describes his fiancée, Theodosia, as a faithless lover:
"your sister," he tells the King of Naples, "That looks like a fair
starre, within loves skie / Is falne, and by the scattering of her fires /

Declares shee has alliance with the earth, / Not heavenly nature"
(IV.i). Later in the same scene the two women, Theodosia with a
dagger in her hand, try to outdo each other in their eagerness to
sacrifice their lives to love. Domitilla exults at the prospect: "My
heart . . . trembles not to be loves martyr; / I can forgive your
hand too, if you promise / To tell the King how willing I die for
him." "The king [!]" exclaims Theodosia, "thou lov'st the Duke."
Domitilla insists, "Hee's not concerned / In my affection; I have no
thought / Of any Prince alive, but your owne brother; / . . . This
he will pardon, shall he know it done / By me more fit to die then
live for him." In an aside Theodosia recognizes a fellow communicant
in the religion of love: "Alas poore Domitilla; shee is wounded / As
deep as I." She begs forgiveness, offers her friendship, and admits,
"There is no cure for love, but love or death." In the Shirley tragedies dramatizing the religion of love, death is indeed the cure;
in the tragicomedies, such as *The Royal Master*, it is love.

In *The Opportunity* love is a tyrant, "more blinde then chance"
for Aurelio-"Borgia" (II.i); it is a matter of life and death, which
"Hange on your lippe" for Ursini, who tells Cornelia, "I come to
be determin'd / Your servant or your sacrifice" (V.i). Marriage to
the woman he loves would bring heaven to earth for Lisimachus in
The Coronation: "What heretofore could happen to mankinde /Was
with much pain to climb to heaven; but in / Sophias marryage of all
Queenes the best, / Heaven will come downe to earth to make me
blest" (I.i). Love creates one soul in bodies twain: "thou / Art all
the joy I have, halfe of my soule" (II.i). Love creates musical harmony for the Duke of Parma in *The Duke's Mistress:* "we will be
Musicke of our selves, / . . . thought of *Ardelia*, / Should strike a
harmony through every heart" (I.i). Love is in harmony with nature:
"Wher's my *Ardelia*? / How at the name my spirits leape within
me, / And the amorous winds doe catch it from my lips / To sweeten
the Ayre—heaven at the sound / Lookes cleare, and lovely, and the
earth put's on / A spring to welcome it." When she appears, "For
whom the World shall weare eternall shine," the Duke addresses
Ardelia as "Brightest *Ardelia*, Queene of love, and me" (ibid.). (See
also, in *The Ball*, IV.iii, "Where union of hearts such Empire
brings, / Subjects, methin[k]s, are crown'd as we[ll] as kings.")
"There is some strange divinity within her," the Duke declares to
Valerio, who irreverently seizes the opportunity for a pun: "I am
not read so farre yet as divinity, / Mine is but human learning"

(ibid.). Possibly this speech is an aside, but it is not so marked; in any case the Duke's ardor is undiminished as he begs Ardelia to

> Speak agen,
> And at thy lipps the quires shall hang to learne
> New tunes, and the dull spheres but coldly imitate,
> I am transform'd with my excesse of rapture.
> Frowne, frowne, *Ardelia,* I shall forget
> I am mortall else, and when thou hast throwne downe
> Thy servant, with one smile exalt agen
> His heart to heaven, and with a kisse breathe in me
> Another soule fit for thy love, but all
> My language is too cold, and we wast time. (Ibid.)

The Duke's declaration of inadequacy in expression of noble sentiments underscores his sincerity; Valerio, the villain of the piece, uses religion-of-love terms (pilgrimage, precious saint) only to mock the holiness of true love.

Leonora in *The Gamester* uses such terms passionately to describe the love of Violante and Beaumont: "Their heart's love hath seald up i'th'eye of Heaven, / 'Twere sacriledge to part 'em" (II.iii). The setting of *The Gamester* is not a foreign court, but London; the main characters are not aristocrats, but commoners. Yet the ladies and gentlemen of the play recognize the sanctity of a true love relationship. In the extension of a contrived and distinctly court-inspired sensibility to middle-class Londoners, Shirley perhaps is suggesting a wider significance for the religion of love than its attractiveness to a privileged coterie.

In one of his wildest city comedies, *The Constant Maid,* the language of the religion of love is replaced by the disease-of-love syndrome. Hartwell complains of love's power and cruelty: "love delights to wound, and see us bleed, / He were a gentle god to kill indeed" (I.i). He considers a drastic cure for his "illness": "Oh, who shall lead me to a world where are / No women? Farewell all! I'll be above / Your charms, and find out death, a cure for love" (III.iv). Mistress Bellamy knows how to feign lovelornness by dwelling on the irrational, extreme nature of love: she loves Hartwell, she says, " 'Bove all the world" (IV.ii); "Love / Hath chang'd both scene and title in our comedy, / And what I meant should shipwrack all his hopes, / Hath ruin'd us" (ibid.). She declares that Hartwell is the "perfect Lover." Her daughter matches her excesses with several expressions of preference for death over living without Hartwell;

like Domitilla in *The Royal Master*, Playfair's cousin reponds to one of the lyrical flights that love inspires with an imploring "No more Raptures." Not daunted, Playfair claims that "love is able, / Without the helpe of sacke, to make a Poet" (IV.iii). For the most part the comic-realistic mode of *The Constant Maid* tends to lighten the solemnity of ritual romantic language.

A similarly realistic tone generally prevails in Shirley's treatment of sexuality. A roistering, bawdy scene in *The Gentleman of Venice* (III.iv) at a house of prostitution features talk of riding, mounting, and tumbling. In *The Gamester* illicit sexual activity requires secrecy: Mistress Wilding chides her husband's page for "closeness" about his master's love affairs (II.i); Wilding arranges an assignation with Penelope with the promise that "all things shall be / So close; no lightning shall peepe in upon us" (III.i). Foscari-Giotto in *The Humourous Courtier* deals with the subject of potency quite graphically: "there's a noise amongst / The Ladies, y'are insufficient: that is, / Your genitalls want the perfect helpe in / Procreation" (IV.i). He is speaking to the humourous courtier Orseola, whose reputation and the way he capitalizes on it anticipate Horner in *The Country Wife*. The medical reference in the following exchange, where Carintha attests to Orseola's "sufficiency" in no uncertain terms, works comically in much the same way as the reference to Horner's collection of porcelain in the "china" scene in Wycherley:

Carintha [referring to Orseola]. He is a rare physitian
Contarini.   He's well skild, in womens pulces.
Carintha.   Theres no feare my Lord,
          But heele recover me, I doe like him infinitely
          For my body, the best in *Padua*.
Contarini.   Good, good, he gave you gentle physicke,
          But you hope twill worke
Carintha.   No *Esculapius*
          Could ha behaved him more judicially.
          Did our Court Ladyes know his skill
          They would be all his Patients, and be sicke a purpose
Contarini.   You hold him then sufficient.
Carintha.   He has a way
          So easie to doe good upon's. (V.i)

Double entendre makes for a sportive tone here, appropriate to a comic treatment of the subject, sex. When dealing with romantic love, Shirley does not neglect sexual attraction, but he usually abandons his sense of humor for a solemn rendition of derivative sentiments. The sentiments expressed about sex in his plays provide occasions for comic invention; those about romantic love, constituting what amounts to an ideology drawn mainly from literary tradition and the alleged practices of the love cult at the court of Henrietta Maria, reveal more concern with coterie taste than with creativity.

At its most extravagant Shirley's language of romantic love has in common with his language of royalism the fanaticism of idolatry and the hyperbole of partisan propaganda. The leading dramatist of Queen Henrietta's acting company catered to his sponsor in terms as inflated as those the fervent patriot reserved for his sovereign. The two vocabularies work together to advance ideals of courtliness whose influence was meant to extend beyond the confines of the court to the kingdom as a whole and even to the cosmos: Shirley's ideal aristocrats perpetuate a vision of permanent order just as his pantheon of ideal lovers rules eternally in a Neo-Platonic universe.

Shirley attributed the highest ideals to the protagonists of plays like *The Young Admiral,* much admired by Sir Henry Herbert, Master of the Revels (licenser of theatrical performances), for its "bettring of maners and language." A year before the production of *The Young Admiral* Sir Henry took exception to *The Ball* for its alleged "personation" of court figures. He insisted on changes before licensing the play for production and threatened "publique punishment" for offending writers and actions. The identification, warranted or not, of Shirley's occasionally unflattering portraits of unworthy lords and ladies with living courtiers accounts for his wavering fortunes at court. Yet no other Caroline playwright reveled more in the rarefied atmosphere of anointed majesty and its attendant splendor.

III   *Wit and Satirist*

Shirley the romantic Royalist would appear to have been at odds with Shirley the city-bred wit who first attracted attention in the theater as the author of the satirical *Love Tricks*. But such an observation overlooks his versatility and adaptability. Today his comedies are considered superior to his tragedies and tragicomedies; in his prefaces and dedications Shirley records public approval of every kind of play he wrote. In any case the targets of satire in the city comedies are not too far removed from the Machiavellian villains in the court plays insofar as the potential for disruption of orderly society is concerned. As a court playwright Shirley usually deals quite solemnly with the ambitious, unscrupulous intriguer; as a Londoner familiar with the aspirations to gentility of the city's middle class he satirizes the *nouveau riche* and the pretentious for irresponsibility or foolishness in their indifference to or ignorance of decorum. The facility with which he could satirize bourgeois social climbers is evident in his first play.

Love Tricks is a merry play about city-dwellers more or less equipped to deal with urban life according to their exercise of wit ("shew thy wit," "let's see thy wit"). Can a foolish old man be foolish enough to be tricked by a city slicker into believing he has been miraculously rejuvenated? Yes, knows Gasparo, a bright young scholar who first displays a zest for satirizing human gullibility in his attack on manufactured news, which unscrupulous pseudojournalists prepare for uncritical readers who believe what they read because they want to believe it. For the same reason Gasparo is able to play upon a foolish and gullible old man's weaknesses. Because Rufaldo is ready to believe that he is young and attractive enough to court and wed a beautiful young virgin, he misses Gasparo's none-too-subtle double entendres: "I have heard some old men have beene twice children sir," or "*Selina* cannot choose but be mad for you" (I.i). Gaspara has no sympathy for gulls. He plays tricks on simpletons for fun and gain.

As if his mentor were Robert Burton, Gasparo's impulse to comic invention arises from a desire to overcome depression: "A pox of Melancholy" he exclaims, grieving over his lost love, Felice. "I have an excellent appetite to make my selfe merry with the simplicity of this age." He embarks on a "project of wit, to make an Asse of the world a little." Thus, "if all hit right, we may / Laugh all our melancholy thoughts away" (I.i). The satirical thrust of the play has a therapeutic intent.

The "low" comedy in *Love Tricks* has Rufaldo and the equally foolish younger Bubulcus carrying on like burlesque comedians in off-color skits. They have much in common not only with their counterparts in Jonson and Shakespeare, but also with latter-day vaudeville comedy teams. Bubulcus and Rufaldo offer each other assurance of attractiveness to the opposite sex; they exchange simpleminded sexual puns ("but where is your daughter, sir? there is no musicke without her, she is the best Instrument to play upon") and lecherous wisecracks ("And you shall have her betweene your

legs, presently"; "I had as liefe be betwixt hers, for all that" [II.i]).
A musician off stage sings a less than accomplished lyric composition
of Rufaldo's celebrating the rejuvenating power of love. This kind
of low comedy has persisted since the seventeenth century in one
form or another of popular entertainment.

Equally durable has been the dominant comic mode of *Love
Tricks*, the "higher," more sophisticated comedy of romantic entanglements, whose exposition makes up most of the first act: Jenkin
is in love with Selina; Gasparo is in love with Felice, who has
disappeared; Infortunio woos Selina in extreme Petrarchan terms,
and she parries his overtures wittily; Antonio loves Hilaria, whose
father, Rufaldo, disapproves of their courtship; and Rufaldo himself
also loves Selina. As in all romantic comedies of whatever era, "true"
lovers (as distinguished from merely "ardent" ones, who are targets
of satire) defeat all opposition, the process involving a minimum of
suspense and, if the playwright is successful, a maximum of fun.

Besides frequent wordplay, the verbal wit of *Love Tricks* features
bawdy expressions of the kind nineteenth-century editors of "the
older drama" described as coarse; dialect humor (Welsh); and parody
of Petrarchism in interpolated songs and in the pseudoromantic
effusions of satirized characters. But even thoughtful lovers, while
not satirized, play their word-games warily, for love itself plays tricks
on lovers. They see love as irrational: in his first speech in the play
Gasparo declares that "Love will make us all mad" (I.i). The words
"mad" and "madness" often accompany general observations and
personal statements about love: "Sure I was mad," says Selina (III.ii),
for spurning young Infortunio and promising to marry old Rufaldo.
The comic language of the play, every variety of wit in it, together
with the expository and the figurative language, simultaneously
works as a means toward "sanity and fulfillment" for successful lovers
and as a comment on a universal human desire over which no degree
of intelligence has much control.

The language pattern of *Love Tricks* is easily discernible: not so
the play's overall structural design. The "School of Complement"
scene (III.v) bears no immediately apparent relationship to the play's
action. The "School" is conceived by a bright young man-about-
town as a temporary relief from melancholy over the disappearance
of the girl he loves. Gasparo hopes to attract would-be gentlemen
and ladies eager to learn the ways and means and words that they
fondly believe will provide the cachet they need to get them into
high society. Except for the "School" scene, *Love Tricks* fulfills the

promise of its title with a series of incidents involving various forms of subterfuge by which three pairs of frustrated lovers are eventually united. Yet external evidence suggests that the "School" scene may have been meant to function on a "metadramatic" level: the first edition of *Love Tricks* in 1631 is entitled *The Schoole of Complement*. In subsequent editions the latter title becomes the subtitle suggested by the original registration of the play as *Love Tricks with Complements*. The "School" scene satirizes false wit, empty rhetoric, and dramatic fustian.

Gasparo as Master of the "School of Complement" and Gorgon (a friend's servant) as his "usher" await customers confidently. Gorgon asks the first, Bubulcus, "does your worship desire to bee sprinkled with the drops of Hellicon, to gather the Pippins of *Pernassus,* and have your forehead fillited with *Apollinean* Bayes, or Laurell?" (III.v). Gasparo and Gorgon overwhelm him with their vocabulary, which is frequently insulting and quite incomprehensible to him. Bubulcus wants to learn how to murder his rival in love with "mouthguns." Delia, a chambermaid, exchanges compliments with Gorgon; the servant of Sir Valentine Wantbrain has Gasparo judge a speech to be delivered in court; Mistress Medulla, another customer, at the "School of Complement" to acquire polish, means to marry into the aristocracy to spite the wife of a justice of the peace in the country; a countryman and "Oaf" arrive for speech training before the son goes to court, where the father has "an offer of five or sixe Offices for my money." A gentleman enters to rant in the manner of Orlando Furioso. Ingeniolo, "a Justice of Peeces Clarke," "speakes his passion in blanke Verse." The Welshman Jenkin comes to learn "Madrigals and Pastoral Canticles." The verses the students learn at Gasparo's school and the compliments they exchange are, unknown to them, quite bawdy. Infortunio enters to talk with the students as if he were Dante interrogating the damned souls in Hell.

This "School of Complement" scene can be related to the play as a whole not only in its satire of clumsy attempts to acquire the graces associated with the nobility, but also in its satire of cultivation for base reasons. The scene and the play appear to have been designed to attack pretension to a way of life to which some are unsuited, such as Jenkin, because of their birth and upbringing; and others, such as Rufaldo, an old man behaving like a young lover, because of their unwillingness or inability to learn, in school or out, what is proper to their age and class.

In the dedication of *Love Tricks* Shirley promises to try in later works for "imaginations of a higher nature," and the prologue presents the author as a fledgling dramatist not to be judged by his "first fruits." He is concerned with order, hierarchy, and artistic development. He develops these concerns by analogies from nature (harvests), from war (victory), from construction (buildings), and from law (inheritance). The play itself reveals in its construction an already settled comic outlook and a firmly grasped technique, involving complicated romantic entanglements; satire of character types modeled mainly on Jonson's; free use of such devices as disguise; and a youthful, enterprising protagonist who projects an image of witty morality and urbane resourcefulness in a contemporary setting as a successful and entertaining contender with prevailing city manners and mores. Gasparo might well have been modeled on Shirley himself.

After his success with *Love Tricks* Shirley wrote at least thirty more plays, including several more city comedies, the best of these representing his finest work in the theater. But a personal note is missing from all his writings after *Love Tricks*, if the Gasparo figure were indeed modeled on the young author as resourceful city-dweller. Shirley established himself in London as leading dramatist for a court-sponsored acting company, devoting himself wholeheartedly for seventeen years after *Love Tricks* to pleasing a fashionable, elitist city audience. All the while he may have yearned for recognition of his literary talent: four years after he stopped writing for the stage there appeared in print poems frequently revised during the twenty-eight years since his first publication, the lost poem *Eccho*. The care Shirley took with the relatively few poems he wrote perhaps represents his bid for literary posterity: plays in his time were considered ephemeral compositions, in spite of reference to them as "poems." Yet the public character of the occasional poems and the conventional themes and tones of the more intimate lyrics reflect, as do the plays after *Love Tricks*, a greater concern for discharging the self-appointed Royalist spokesman's responsibilities to maintenance of the status quo than for exploring disinterestedly the seventeenth century's challenging intellectual and artistic innovations.

IV *Poet and Playwright*

Shirley's first publication, *Eccho, or the Infortunate Lovers,* a poem in the classical amatory vein of Marlowe's *Hero and Leander* and Shakespeare's *Venus and Adonis,* appeared in 1618. Although no copy of the poem is extant, it is generally considered to be the same as *Narcissus, or The Self-Lover,* included in *Poems &c by James Shirley* (1646). Except for commendatory verses for other writers' works, nothing besides *Eccho* of Shirley's nondramatic verse was published until 1646; indeed, *Poems &c* is the only such collection in his lifetime. The plays were published singly, beginning with *The Wedding* in 1629, but no complete edition of Shirley's works appeared until the nineteenth century.

The size of the canon is comparable to that of Shakespeare's. In addition to a modest amount of nondramatic verse, Shirley wrote at least four tragedies, eight tragicomedies, eight romantic comedies, and a dozen or more comedies of manners. These do not include lost plays, plays of doubtful authorship sometimes attributed to Shirley, or other writers' plays that he revised.[24] Shirley had a very disciplined attitude toward his work, if regularity of production is a reliable indicator. Bentley lists Shirley among the eight most prolific playwrights of the period 1590–1642.[25] Playwriting was a lucrative profession for Shirley, who "took in more cash" from his "professional activities than was usual for writers."[26] Playwriting was the source of his income from 1625 to 1642. He owed his success to favorable response to his depiction in comedies of fashionable London life and to his evocation of aristocratic ideals in his tragedies and tragicomedies.

Not all Caroline theater was an appendage of the court party. The upper classes patronized the Phoenix, Blackfriars, and Salisbury Court theaters, with the Globe, Fortune, and Red Bull "reserved to the rank-scented many."[27] As a rule the "private" theaters offered one play a week to audiences made up primarily of noblemen and their ladies, and secondarily of professionals, such as lawyers and the more expensive prostitutes of the day. The "public" theaters catered to every class in daily performance. The soberer middle-class citizens, not necessarily all Puritans, had been at least indifferent and at most hostile to plays and playhouses since Elizabethan times.[28] They were not likely to patronize either public or private theaters in Shirley's time. Shirley wrote for the private theaters, except toward the end of his career. The Globe audience he addressed in the prologue to *The Doubtful Heir* was not hostile to theater, but Shirley had written the play originally for an Anglo-Irish audience in Dublin, and he was worried about its reception on the "Banckside."

The Globe audience, socially inferior to the one at the Blackfriars, was alien to the Shirley who had his Prologue say:

> Our Author did not calculate this Play
> For this Meridian; the Banckside, he knows,
> Are far more skilfull at the Ebbes and flows
> Of water, than of wit, he did not mean
> For the elevation of your poles, this scene.

The "poles" refer to the means of ferrying passengers and freight up and down the Thames, on whose banks the Globe was situated. The theater's largely lower-middle-class and working-class audience, says the Prologue, would not find in *The Doubtful Heir* the kind of spectacle they were used to seeing at the Globe: "No shews, no dance, . . . no target fighting," and instead of salacious jokes and indecent songs ("No bawdery, nor no Ballets"), the play offers "language clean." Moreover, the action of the play would not strain credulity ("Without impossibilities the Plot"). The characters include "No clown, no squibs, no Devill." Shirley has the Prologue advise the audience to sit "As you were now in the Black-Fryers pit," and he hopes they "will not deaf us, with leud noise and tongues." The play is "meant for your persons, not the place." The dedication in the first edition of *The Doubtful Heir* in 1652 speaks of the "estimation it gained" in its "active representment," probably referring to the Globe production in 1640. So the audience then may not have taken offense at the Prologue or at a production without the fireworks, real and metaphorical, allegedly popular at the Globe.

Even when he was writing exclusively for upper-class audiences at the private theaters, Shirley must have had doubts about the quality of his work. Theatrical conventions of the Caroline period that exaggerated the importance of spectacle on stage restricted the kind of playwrights who a generation before might have ventured to write a worthy "poem for the scene." Not too subtly Shirley lets it be known that much of what he writes for the Caroline stage must meet the demands of a debased taste in his audiences. The poetaster

Caperwit in *Changes* proposes the production of a masque to a dancer with reference to the way musical spectacle has become an important feature of stage plays:

> Oh Sir, what Playes are taking without these
> Pretty devices? Many Gentlemen
> Are not, as in the dayes of understanding,
> Now satisfied without a Jigge which since
> They cannot, with their honour, call for, after
> The play, they looke to be serv'd up ith' middle:
> Your dance is the best language of some Comedies,
> And footing runs away with all; a Scene
> Expresst with life of Art, and squar'd to nature,
> Is dull and flegmatick Poetry. (IV.ii)

The last speech of the masque that ends *Changes* has the most melancholy of its characters step out of character to advertise the new little (small) theater for which Shirley wrote the play. *Changes* includes much internal evidence of Shirley's struggles to write successfully for the stage; in dedications, prologues, epilogues, and commendatory verses or critical prefaces to other writers' works, he reveals rather appealingly his desire to write well.

In the dedication of *The Young Admiral* to Lord Berkley, Shirley expresses the hope that this "Poeme" will be accepted until he can offer "something of more high endeavour." Often referring to a play as a "poem," Shirley sought "excellency in the Musicall Arte of Poesie" (*The Wedding*, Dedication). Defending "unbefriended poesy," the Prologue to *The Example* claims that "poets now . . . suffer for their guilt of truth, and arts." Shirley tried to avoid obscurity: there was "no language good / And artful, but what's clearly understood"; "the language here is cleare" (*The Coronation*, Prologue); and he eschewed obscenity: "Our Author hath no guilt of scurrill [scenes]" (*The Duke's Mistress*, Prologue). According to the epilogue to *The Doubtful Heir* the audience might reasonably ask of a play: "Is the Plot current? may we trust the wit," and "Are the lines Sterling? do they hold conceit?" The Prologue to *St. Patrick for Ireland* wishes the audience "Knew but the art and labour of a Play; / Then you would value the true Muses paine, / The throws and travell of a teeming braine." Looking back after thirteen years away from the stage, Shirley writes in 1655 (*The Politician*, Dedication) that the "language" of "dramatique recreations . . . glorified the English Scene" (i.e., the stage) at a time when "the common

Theaters . . . were not so happily purg'd from scurrility, and under-wit, (the onely entertainment of vulgar Capacities)."

No one had "glorified the English scene" more than Ben Jonson ("our acknowledg'd Master, learned JONSON," *The Grateful Serv-ant*, Dedication). Jonson, an Elizabethan original in more ways than one, had been a leading playwright since the beginning of the century, one of three major Elizabethan dramatists whose careers spanned the Jacobean period into the Caroline. Three years after Jonson's death in 1637, when Shirley produced *The Alchemist* in Dublin, he wrote a prologue that includes such phrases as "true art," "masterpiece," and "poets' king."[29] He recognized Jonson as an innovator and an authentic genius. His admiration for Beaumont and Fletcher was almost equally great: "the best wit ever trod the English stage."[30] The "sort of tragicomedy" represented by *Philaster* "provided the main pattern for plays by Shirley."[31]

If today Beaumont and Fletcher's and Shirley's tragicomedies and romantic comedies seem farfetched and remote from real life, in the 1620s and 1630s their stock in trade (disguises, forced marriages, illicit romantic liaisons and intrigues) drew as much from the more sensational escapades of Caroline aristocracy as from tried-and-true melodramatic stage formulae. Consider the adventures of Frances Coke, "the victim of an enforced match" with Sir John Villiers, whom she left "to live in adultery with Sir Robert Howard." Coke twice avoided doing public penance "by the same means as the heroines of many a romantic comedy." She escaped arrest in 1627 and prison in 1634 by disguising herself as a boy. A convert to Roman Catholicism in France, "she was pardoned by Charles I and permitted to return to England" in 1640.[32] Charles himself might have been the model for the hero of a stage adventure: he met Henrietta Maria in Paris at a court ballet rehearsal (at which they scarcely noticed each other) during as contrived and romantic a journey as any in one of Shirley's "disguise" plots. To court the Infanta Doña Maria of Spain, Charles "left London incognito . . . as Jack Smith on February 17, 1623."[33] The project was the idea of the Duke of Buckingham, who traveled as "Tom Smith." Charles's father, King James I, referred to the two young men (both of whom wore false beards) as "Dear Sweet boys, worthy to be put into a new Romanso."[34] After the breakdown of negotiations for the Span-ish alliance, Charles learned that Henrietta Maria was pleased with a miniature portrait of him. Their ultimate marriage may have been arranged for reasons of state, but as theatrically romantic lovers they rivaled Princess Leonora and the Duke of Savoy in *The Grateful Servant* and Eugenia and Philenzo in *The Bird in a Cage*. As for intrigue, Henrietta's machinations (unsuccesssful long-distance attempts to oust her brother Louis XIII's favorite, Cardinal Richelieu) matched those of Queen•Marpisa in *The Politician* and of the Duchess Rosaura in *The Cardinal*.

Thus, while Caroline drama often seems to belong to a world of fantasy, a small part of the real world provided enough glamour and excitement to stimulate the imaginations of some playwrights of the time. Not all of them: Ben Jonson, whose imagination was vivid enough to create the fantastic humor characters in a series of city comedies that established him as the leading playwright of the Jacobean era, continued to write after Charles came to the throne, but his late plays and masques failed to win approval because he insisted on strong doses of unrestricted realism in them.

Echoes of Jonson, Beaumont and Fletcher, and other English and Continental poets and playwrights of the sixteenth and seventeenth centuries sound throughout Shirley's work.[35] Striking similarities may be noted between *The Lady of Pleasure* and John Fletcher's *The Wild-Goose Chase*, or between *The Cardinal* and John Webster's *The Duchess of Malfi*. Peregrine, Fitzavarice, and Lady Peregrine in *The Example* form a triangle much like that of Auria, Adurni, and Spinella in John Ford's *The Lady's Trial*. Haraldus in *The Politician* echoes Hamlet in a confrontation with his mother:

Marpisa.	Th'art dejected;
	Have but a will and live.
Haraldus.	'Tis in vaine, mother.
Marpisa.	Sink with a feavour into earth?
	Look up, thou shalt not dye.
Haraldus.	I have a wound within
	You do not see, more killing than all feavors.(IV.iii)

Gotharus in the same play expresses boundless ambition in accents reminiscent of Marlowe's Tamburlaine, but Gotharus's motives are different: he intrigues for love as well as for power, and he gains his ends by plots, not by risking his life on a battlefield. Angellina, Contarini, and Pulcheria in disguise as Vergerio in *The Sisters* recall Olivia, the Duke, and Viola in *Twelfth Night;* the steward Lucio and Piperollo, Malvolio and Feste. One of Montalto's speeches in *The Royal Master* (II.ii) sounds like a Shakespearean sonnet. Ferochus and Endarius in *St. Patrick for Ireland* recall the boys in *Cymbeline*. Torn between love and honor, Vittori in *The Young Admiral* offers a variation on a familiar couplet by Lovelace: "How canst thou hope I should preserve my faith / Unstain'd to thee, and breake to all the world?" (III.i). If there is a borrowing here, Lovelace was indebted to Shirley for the sentiment, for the play was written in the 1630s and "To Lucasta: Going to the Wars," in the 1640s. But the love-versus-honor conflict was certainly not original with Shirley.[36]

Shirley shared with contemporary playwrights the themes, characters, and situations of Elizabethan and Jacobean plays that had become standard theater fare in the Caroline period.[37] However, a similarity in the content or structure of scenes of London life in Shirley's city comedies to those of his contemporaries or predecessors does not necessarily indicate influence or model. Shirley knew his man-in-the-street's London at first hand, including some distinctly plebeian haunts. The London landmarks referred to in such diverse works as *A Contention for Honour and Riches*, *The Ball*, *The Constant Maid*, *The Gamester*, and *Honoria and Mammon* cover an extensive geographical range in every direction.[38] Shirley in fact writes most confidently when the setting is contemporary London. The plays with foreign settings are generally less imaginatively conceived, surprisingly perhaps, and more dependent on literary sources.

Plays of whatever setting frequently allude to current English interests, such as America. During Shirley's lifetime English colonization of America began; nothing in Shirley's work suggests any personal interest in the project: in *A Contention*, for example, Riches declares, "Though my name / Be Riches, yet my mother was a *Clod*, / She married rich earth of America, / Where I was borne, a durty family, / But many matches have refined us now, / And we are called *Riches*." America clearly figures in Shirley's mind, as in most Englishmen's of his time, as a raw, crude source of wealth for the Mother Country.[39] *The Opportunity* refers to the Thirty Years' War, then (1634) in progress, and to the temper of the Spanish. England was not involved in this war between Sweden and Germany, but Spain's active support of Austria and the German states during the early years of the war had ruined the late King James's hopes of an alliance through marriage of Prince Charles to the Spanish Infanta; moreover, Spain's continuing threat to the English Channel as the strength of the English navy (the country's main bulwark against the

Spanish since the 1580s) steadily declined must have troubled all Englishmen, including Shirley.

Perhaps most significant in this context of national concern is the prologue to *The Sisters*, the last play of Shirley's to be produced before the closing of the theaters in 1642. The prologue takes account of the current state of affairs in England: "Our Poet thinks the whole Town is not well," for even though the theaters have not yet closed, attendance has fallen off dramatically. With Charles's flight (*"London is gone to York"*) in 1642 "the whole Town . . . dares not salute this Ayr." The prologue includes a lament for the neglect by Londoners of plays by Shakespeare, Fletcher, and Jonson ("t'whose name, wise Art did bow"). King, country, city, and civilization itself are in jeopardy. Shirley's theatrical career, resumed so auspiciously less than two years earlier on his return from Ireland, when he became principal writer for the King's Men in succession to Shakespeare, Fletcher, and Massinger (d. 1640), was now (1642) at an end.

CHAPTER 2

"Will Your Grace See a Song?": Masques and Nondramatic Verse

SHIRLEY'S celebration of Royalist style and taste, discernible even in the plays with middle-class settings and characters, achieves its most egregious expression in masque, a bizarre theatrical hybrid peculiar to the Stuart period. Spectacle was the *raison d'être* of Stuart masque, which supposedly served the same moral-didactic purpose as the early Tudor interlude. Adding gorgeous, often fantastic, costumes, settings, properties, and singing and dancing shifted the emphasis to elaborate staging. Stuart masque primarily served a social and ceremonial purpose in combining professional and amateur talents for extravagant exercises in pageantry (the cast, unlike its Tudor predecessor, included courtiers and Inns of Court students). The curious mélange constituted an exotic divertissement designed for a predominantly courtly audience; the splendor of production glorified the Crown.

Considering his devotion to royalism, Shirley manifests an uncharacteristically ambivalent attitude toward masque in several of his plays and even in his greatest achievement in the genre, *The Triumph of Peace*, which exploits spectacle and incidentally ridicules the taste for it. On the one hand, Shirley pays tribute in *Love's Cruelty* to Inigo Jones for the glamour and beauty of masque production:

Are you Melancholy? a Maske is prepared, and Musicke to charme *Orpheus* himselfe into a stone, numbers presented to your eare that shall speake the soule of the immortall English *Jonson,* a scene to take your eye with wonder, now to see a forrest move, and the pride of summer brought into a walking wood, in the instant, as if the sea had swallowed up the earth, to see waves capering about tall ships, *Arion* upon a rocke playing to the Dolphins, the *Tritons* calling up the sea Nimphes, to dance before you: in the height of this rapture a tempest so artificiall and sudden in the clouds, with a generall darkenes and thunder so seeming made to threaten, that you would cry out with the Marriners in the worke, you cannot scape drowning, in the turning of an eye, these waters ravish [vanish?] into a heaven, glorious and angelicall shapes presented, the starres distinctly with their motion and musick so inchanting you, that you would wish to be drowned indeed, to dwell in such a happinesse. (II.ii)

Certainly *The Triumph of Peace* was a great success in its time (several years after the production of *Love's Cruelty;* Shirley is clearly referring to a Jonson masque in this passage), and Shirley would rightly credit Inigo Jones for that success.

On the other hand, we may infer from a passage in *The Royal Master* that Shirley had a low opinion of masque production immediately before the outbreak of the Civil War. (Actually *The Royal Master* may have been written as early as 1636, for it is one of the plays that belong to Shirley's "Irish" period, 1636-40; it was certainly written some time after the success of *The Triumph of Peace*.) Bombo and Iacomo in the following excerpt are minor characters in *The Royal Master:*

Bombo. I may have a humour to make a Maske if they
       Stay supper.
Iacamo.   Thou make a Maske.
Bombo. I doe not say Ile write one, for I ha' not
       My writing tongue, though I could once have read,
       But I can give if neede be the designe,
       Make worke among the Deale boards, and perhaps
       Can teach 'em as good language as another
       Of competent ignorance; things goe not now
       By learning; I have read 'tis but to bring
       Some pretty impossibilities, for Antemaskes
       A little sense and wit dispos'd with thrift,
       With here and there Monsters to make 'em laugh:
       For the grand businesse to have *Mercury*
       Or *Venus Dandeprat* to usher in
       Some of the gods that are good fellowes dancing,
       Or goddesses, and now and then a song,
       To fill a gap; a thousand crownes, perhaps,
       For him that made it, and theres all the wit. (II.i)

Since he wrote masque himself and employed many of the devices satirized above (including the "grand businesse" introduced by

"Venus Dandeprat," Cupid), Shirley may well have been poking fun at himself, too.

Shirley's contribution to masque conformed to prevailing taste. The literary content of Stuart masque was most often slight; only rarely did nondramatic writers attempt masque. Milton wrote his as a favor for a friend, but used the opportunity to emphasize the lesser consideration. Among the works of Shirley's other contemporaries, the text of Thomas Carew's *Coelum Britannicum* (like *Comus* and *Arcades* set to music by Henry Lawes) is an important part of the poet's oeuvre, elsewhere equally indebted to Donne and Jonson. Jonson, the master of the form, manipulated the operatic elements of masque well enough to make even the libretto and stage directions on the printed page as coherent as a staged performance could have been in his time.[1]

Shirley's approach to masque was little different from that to drama. His impulse toward allegory governs characterization throughout his work, whether he is creating abstract figures for masque proper, morality play, masque as play-within-a-play, or type-characters for drama. His theatrical taste required at least elementary coherence, even though, like Carew and Davenant, and unlike Jonson, he left all the production details to Inigo Jones.[2] And his practice of using the theater to advance the Royalist cause meant that he would find the didactic character of masque congenial. In all his work Shirley's special pleading determines not only the intellectual level of discourse, but also the course of the narrative (invariably moving toward a reassertion of aristocratic ideals) and the nature of the characterization (by type, according to a strict Royalist code of social ethics). Study of the masques, moral allegories, and nondramatic verse proves rewarding for the light they throw on Shirley's aesthetic, moral-philosophical, and sociopolitical principles as these inform conduct of action in the plays: theater experience as ritual, stage action as parable, dramatic dianoia as polemic.

I *Masques and Moral Allegories*

The Inns of Court commissioned Shirley to write his first masque, *The Triumph of Peace*. The occasion was the association of lawyers' desire to demonstrate loyalty to the Crown: the production would offset William Prynne's alleged criticism of the queen in *Histrio-mastix,* to which Shirley had already responded in a mock-dedication of *The Bird in a Cage* to Prynne. The Inns of Court presented masques as a substantial part of the cultural program for the student body. Theatrical activities included play production and such related entertainments as "revels." The students also danced, jousted, and participated in the pageantry of the "pre-masque procession of about two hundred masquers and gentlemen of the Inns of Court through the streets of London" which "terminated at the Banqueting House, where the masque was then performed."[3]

Shirley's association with the Inns of Court may have begun as early as 1625 on his arrival in London, if it is true that he took up residence at the family quarters available at Gray's Inn. He appears to have been eager to identify himself as belonging to the society. He interrupted the 1633 printing of *The Triumph of Peace* to include "Invented and Written, By James Shirley, of Grayes Inne, Gent." on the title page. "This alteration was probably occasioned by the author's desire that it should be known that he was a member of one of the societies which presented the masque and not a mere hired hack."[4]

Shirley's pride in the sponsorship of *The Triumph of Peace* by the Inns of Court was matched by his pride in the august audience that the masque attracted. He describes the audience in the preface to the first edition of *The Triumph of Peace*: "This Masque was presented in the *Banqueting-House*. At white Hall, before the *King* and *Queenes* Majesties and a great Assembly of *Lords* and *Ladies*, and other persons of quality, whose aspect setting on the degrees prepared for that purpose, gave a great grace to this spectacle, especially being all richly attired." The image of a splendid assembly like this one figures forth Shirley's ideas of political order, as it did Jonson's.[5] No more of Shirley's masques were to be presented before the king and queen. Even in 1633 they must have found the mild satire of some aspects of court life in *The Triumph of Peace* innocuous: the glorification in the masque of their royal counterparts, Jove and Themis, underscored the essential role monarchy played in maintaining order. Disorder, the essential antimasque element in *The Triumph of Peace*, thrives at court only temporarily, and then only with the indulgence of the monarch.

The Triumph of Peace opens with Opinion and Confidence (like the two courtiers, often unnamed, at the beginning of Shirley's court plays, who are responsible for the necessary exposition) discussing the arrival at court of Fancy. With his companions Jollity and Laughter, Fancy receives a warm welcome from Opinion, Confidence, and Opinion's wife, Novelty, and daughter Admiration. Fancy is appalled to learn that no antimasques are scheduled and proceeds to present one, the first in a series of rowdy scenes. At a tavern another antimasque is performed by its Master, his Wife, and servants; a Maquerelle (bawd), two Wenches, two Gamesters; a Gentleman and four Beggars who feign crippling until they receive alms from the Gentleman. In turn enter to dance a Jockey, a Country-Fellow, and a series of six Projectors (one has invented a double-boiler; another, deep-sea diving gear); an agriculturist; and a shipwright. Maquerelle, the Wenches, and the Gentleman dance; the Gamester dances.

The scene shifts to a Woodland, with Owl, Crow, Kite, Jay, Magpie, all dancers, followed by a Merchant a'Horseback, two Thieves, a Constable and Officers; then enter Nymphs, Satyrs, and four Huntsmen who chase away the Satyrs and dance with the Nymphs. The scene shifts again to one featuring Dotterels (easily caught birds). The next has a Knight, a Squire, and a Windmill in a parody of *Don Quixote*. All the characters go off stage as Irene (Peace) descends in a chariot. Eunomia (Law) comes next, then Diche (Justice). They sing an ode to the enthroned Jove and Themis. Sixteen sons of Irene present a masque with a Genius, which ends with Hours and Chori singing, interrupted by a Carpenter and others. Then the Masquers sing, and the scene shifts again to the country and Amphiluche (forerunner of the morning), a singer; offstage voices sing the last song, and Genius steps to the front of the stage to compliment King Charles and Queen Henrietta.

The libretto of *The Triumph of Peace* occupies little more space on the printed page than the stage directions, yet the negligible narrative line (if the course of the "action" may be so described) traces a fairly distinct moral-didactic pattern. Phansie [Fancy] introduces the theme of peace with the tavern scene. Opinion considers the spectacle corrupt and the crippled beggars undesirable "effects of peace"; Phansie claims they "shew / The benefit of peace." Until the entrance of Irene Phansie's noisy antimasques oppose the two points of view—Phansie's of peace as making possible freedom from all restraint; Opinion's of such irresponsible indulgence as license. The "sons of Peace" (as Genius refers in the epilogue to the members of the Inns of Court), as guardians of law and justice, serve the spirit of peace in helping bring order out of chaos. The latter scenes of the masque illustrate the way freedom of the imagination can be exercised responsibly. The sober speeches of Eunomia and Diche preserve the solemnity of the occasion.

Shirley's second masque, *The Triumph of Beauty*, deals with a classical myth Shirley had already dramatized in short masque sequences in two of his plays. In a grove Bottle and several other shepherds discuss ways to relieve their prince Paris's melancholy, and decide on a production of the Tragedy of the Golden Fleece. Paris enters to soliloquize dolefully on his banishment for dreaming and to submit to the shepherds' entertainment. He falls asleep. Mercury descends to announce Paris's selection as judge among Juno, Cytherea, and Pallas. He has to choose among wealth and power, wisdom and courage, love and beauty. He gives the golden ball to Cytherea. After Juno and Pallas leave, Cytherea's son, blind Cupid, enters to sing and dance with Hymen, Delight, Graces, and Hours (Eunomia, Diche, and Irene again) in celebration of the triumph of beauty and love.

This "private entertainment," designed for a very small, select audience, reads more like a play than does *The Triumph of Peace*. Only the Bottle scenes may be gratuitous, for none of the shepherds appears in the last third of the action. (Their counterparts in *A Midsummer Night's Dream* at least receive some acknowledgment from Theseus for their efforts.) Still, the narrative line is slightly stronger than that of *Peace*, the speeches longer, and the moral clearer: "Love dwells with beauty, they together move; / There is no beauty where there is not love." The sentiment is as far removed from political realities as that of *Peace* thirteen years earlier was involved in them. Staged in 1646, *The Triumph of Beauty* must be recognized as essentially escapist, as Shirley's third and last masque, *Cupid and Death*, is not.

During the Commonwealth period masque was not specifically proscribed, but there are records of only a few performances for special state occasions. *Cupid and Death*, with music by Matthew Locke and Christopher Gibbons, was staged three times, first in 1653, as a government-sponsored project. It was first published in March of the same year and reprinted in 1659.[6] The narrative line is, again, a little less frantic than that of *The Triumph of Peace;* the moral it points is much more relevant to the political realities of the 1650s than that of *The Triumph of Beauty* to those of the 1640s.

In the opening scene a tavernkeeper (Host) and Chamberlain await the arrival of "immortal guests" Cupid and Death. Cupid enters attended by Folly and Madness; the Host and Chamberlain join them in song and dance. When the five leave, Death enters; the Chamberlain reappears to welcome him. Then Despair comes in, apparently to capitulate to Death, but changes his mind after a drink of wine. Meanwhile the Chamberlain has fallen asleep; by the time he awakes, Death and his train have gone. The scene shifts to a garden where ladies lament lovers slain by Cupid. Nature, old cripples, armed gentlemen, the Chamberlain, two apes, a Satyr, and Mercury figure in the ensuing spectacle.

The most interesting feature of the action is the banishment of the Chamberlain from court: he is assigned to poor people's houses. Near the beginning of the masque he had described the irresponsible behavior of drunken wastrels: "These rantings were the badges of our gentry. / But all their dancing days are done, I fear." *Cupid and Death* is clearly a product of the Interregnum.

Shirley also published a moral allegory during the Commonwealth period, *The Contention of Ajax and Ulysses for the Armour of Achilles*, designed as a private entertainment for young gentlemen of quality, according to the title page. More declamatory than dramatic, this work served as an educational project for Shirley's "young gentlemen" pupils. The all-male cast of characters and the prominence of two clever young pages among the legendary Homeric heroes mark this piece as a special composition for Shirley's students at Whitefriars in the 1650s.

The Contention is made up of three short scenes. In the first, Lysippus and Didymus, pages to Ajax and Ulysses, respectively, quarrel near the tent of Agamemnon. Calchas enters to stop them and announce the contention. Officers enter with Achilles' armor, then Agamemnon, Nestor, Menelaus, Diomedes, Thersander, and others, and, finally, Ajax and Ulysses, who gets the armor. In the second scene, Lysippus and Didymus make up (Ajax has run away mad), and together decide to make fun of Polybrontes, who claims to be a son of Hercules and takes credit for all the heroes' victories over the Trojans. Ajax returns to beat him, and Polybrontes runs off. Calchas enters to assure Ajax that the gods are on his side, that he will receive the armor when he dies. Ajax goes off stage to commit suicide. The last scene is the shortest: Calchas sings "The glories of our blood and state" before Ajax's body, and Agamemnon grieves briefly for the dead hero. The play ends with the couplet "Joys are abortive, or not born to last, / And our bright days are quickly overcast." Ajax's death has made the Greeks' "day of triumph" dark in their calendar. *The Contention* is best remembered, if at all, for

Calchas's song at the end, often cited without reference to the play itself.

Another moral allegory, *A Contention for Honour and Riches*, written in 1632, but not produced in Shirley's lifetime, served as a first draft for *Honoria and Mammon* (1658-59). *A Contention for Honour and Riches* moves in its three scenes from the palace of Lady Riches to the house of Honour and then outside, near the two residences. *Honoria and Mammon*, an "elaboration and expansion of the author's *A Contention for Honour and Riches*,"[7] is made up of five acts (fourteen scenes). The occasion was another academic exercise for Shirley's pupils in the 1650s and 1660s.

Despite the allegorical names of the characters, *Honoria and Mammon* reads more like Shirley's earlier city comedies than like the *Ajax and Ulysses*. Aurelia, wealthy widow of Sir Omnipotent Mammon, refuses financial aid or a position in her household to the scholar Alworth, who serves Honoria. Aurelia is courted by the citizen Fulbank and the countryman Maslin, whom her gentleman-usher Phantasm gives swords for dueling. The courtier Alamode and Colonel Conquest court Honoria, too. When Alworth arrives with a report of Aurelia's response to his request, Honoria is not surprised. Alone, Alamode and the Colonel have a brief duel.

Phantasm gulls Fulbank into settling his estate on Mammon through the lawyer Traverse, who serves both Honoria and Mammon. Honoria places a wreath on Alworth, in whom "do meet / The courtier and the soldier" (II.ii), but removes it when he bursts into ecstatic fulsomeness, punctuated by classical allusions. He faints when he discovers he is still in her favor. In the third act Traverse seems to have won Mammon, to the displeasure of Fulbank and the delight of Maslin. Phantasm suggests to Traverse that he court Honoria. Alworth and Phantasm kick Dash, Traverse's servant, as they tell him Alworth will marry Mammon. Traverse himself tells Honoria that Alworth has died.

The citizens of "Metropolis" hire the Colonel and Captain Squandering to conduct a civil war that will retrieve Mammon from Traverse. Mammon comes to marry Maslin, but tells Alamode to stay. The Colonel and the rebels capture Fulbank, Traverse, and Dash. Alworth, alive and disguised, is taken into custody by the Colonel and Captain Squandering. The rebels also capture Mammon, and Phantasm vanishes. Now the Colonel has both Honoria and Mammon. Honoria visits Alworth in prison. Traverse refuses the Colonel's suggestion that he shoot Alworth: law and learning are restored to honor; the Colonel will serve them nobly, as Mammon will serve Honoria, for the Colonel and Mammon are in love. The play ends with Alworth and Honoria going off to marry.

Honoria and Mammon satirizes rather ponderously the pursuit of wealth to the neglect of honor and learning, with incidental harsh comment on the decay of urban society, dishonorable military men, greedy citizenry, and crude country manners. As if the allegory were not clear enough, Shirley includes several superfluous glosses on the action, such as "Honour is the lustre of all triumph, / The glories that we wear are dim without her" (V.i). Study of *Honoria and Mammon* and of Shirley's other works in its and related genres is instructive about the puzzlingly static quality of some of Shirley's last plays. Not that the masques and moralities are made up exclusively of solemn dicta and lifeless abstractions: the moralities have swift and clear narrative action and frequently witty dialogue; both the moralities and the masques have occasional neatly phrased and measured lyrics. Yet they lack the dramatic urgency that a morality play can have. *Everyman* invests some of its abstract characters with human complexity; the wit, the course of the action, and the verse are thereby integrated in a comic (but not irreverent), essentially dramatic treatment of a solemn theme. Honoria and Mammon and the other characters in Shirley's morality play remain abstractions; Shirley adds wit, action, and verse solemn and comic to produce a mixture, not a blend. In studying pieces like *Honoria and Mammon*, one may come to understand that Shirley often employs his skill as a playwright arbitrarily, to make a moral lesson palatable. Conflict thus becomes superficial, illustrating specific deviations from a strict code of social morality. In such works Shirley's mastery of playwriting technique mainly serves the cause of undemanding theatrical entertainment, with a little schoolbook enlightenment thrown in for good measure.

II *Masque as Play-within-a-Play*

Shirley uses masque as play-within-a-play for generally didactic and specifically dramatic purposes. In the third act of *The Traitor* Sciarrha, apparently to thank the Duke for favors, arranges a ballet that is really intended to remind him of what would happen if he succeeded in seducing Sciarrha's sister. Luxury, accompanied by the Pleasures, boasts of his triumph over Love in the hearts of the great. Sciarrha provides the Duke with a running moral commentary on the action involving a wealthy young man who is seized first by Luxury and Pleasure and then by Death and the Furies. Shirley manages a clever structural integration of this brief spectacle about lust and death, for it is paralleled in the last act by the Duke's lustful embrace of what proves to be a corpse.

In *The Coronation,* a play conceived as a dramatic demonstration of the natural superiority of the nobly born (whose true identity may be hidden only temporarily), the contribution of the masque sequence to the development of the theme figures more subtly. The masque in *The Coronation* is designed to touch the conscience of an unfaithful lover. Fortune, crowned like a queen, accompanied by Youth, Health, and Pleasure, appears in the house of Love, whom Fortune charms with dancing cupids. Honour suddenly appears to reclaim Love. The noble heart, dazzled by delusive outward circumstance, need only be reminded of its innate dignity to be saved from an ignoble, dishonorable alliance.

Masque as an appurtenance of a royal court becomes, rather perfunctorily, a significant part of the climactic action in *The Cardinal,* for here Shirley makes no attempt to relate the content of the masque, truncated for plot purposes, to the play's theme. The incomplete spectacle functions as a plot device: Columbo arranges to have murderers disguised as masquers kill his rival; the scene involves dancing, described in the stage directions, but no songs for the performers. Masque in *The Cardinal* does not interrupt or comment on the action, but advances it. Similarly, the masque sequence in the fourth act of *The Constant Maid* is interspersed with commentary by characters in the main action of the play. The masque itself is limited to dance and mime. It advances the plot in revealing a secret marriage between two of the masquers, playing Paris and his bride, led in by Venus and Cupid after Paris has rejected offers from Juno and Pallas.

That Caroline dramatists considered a masque sequence almost mandatory probably accounts for its presence in *The Ball.* Shirley contrives again to integrate it thematically. That the golden ball of the masque in the last act refers not only to the one Paris gave Venus but also to the ball (dance) of the title is clear from Venus's first speech:

> this meeting is
> To ruffle Ladies, and to kisse,
> These are my Orgies, from each eye,

A thousand wanton glances flie;
Lords, and Ladies of the Game,
Each brest be full of my owne flame. . . . (V.i)

But Venus is as mistaken about the nature of "these revels" as she is about the "Lords, and Ladies of the Game" attending them: Diana defies her with the claim that "These are none of *Venus* traine." The play, corrective in its intent, works to set the record straight on a briefly notorious and perhaps undeservedly maligned social event of the early 1630s in London, a ball rumored to be the occasion for arranging assignations among members of London society. Similarly, the masque in the last scene of the play turns the old Greek myth upside down. Diana is the winner of the golden ball, for Cupid abandons his mother, throws away his "licentious shafts," and embraces "chast" love. Just as the play reveals that the annual London ball is an innocent affair, so the masque upsets popular notions of what really happened on "*Ida* hill."

In *Changes* more interesting than the masque itself [8] or its relationship to the rest of the play is the Caperwit speech (IV.ii), where Shirley may be describing his own practice, for even in plays without masques, stage directions call for interpolation of song, dance, or instrumental music. "Musician sings within" (*Love Tricks*, II.i); "One sings within" (*The Witty Fair One*, IV.iii); "Song above" (*The Opportunity*, II.i): such stage directions suggest the pervasiveness of the practice. Sometimes lyrics accompany these, sometimes not. *St. Patrick for Ireland*, which has more songs than any other Shirley play, includes several short masquelike scenes: a religious ceremony in the second act; ghostly apparitions dancing in the third; a blood-sacrifice in a pagan temple in the fourth. The last scene of *Love Tricks* features garlanded shepherds and shepherdesses singing on a "shepherds' holiday" in praise of Pan, their patron deity. The stage directions following the song read: "*Dance. The Song ended, Enter a Maske of Satyres &c.*, and dance, *Enter a Shepherdess with a white rod.*" Another song ends the revelry. The length of the entire sequence on stage would depend on the time devoted to dancing; the two songs are short. The sequence as a whole occupies only a single page of print. *The Grateful Servant*, which also has no formal masque, interpolates a short scene of singing and dancing satyrs and nymphs, who are to lead the "wild and lascivious" Lodwick to what he thinks will be an assignation. The nymphs reappear briefly at the beginning of the next scene, before Lodwick discovers he has been duped (IV.iv, v).

Curiously, *The Bird in a Cage,* the kind of Caroline extravaganza that would easily accommodate a masque sequence, features instead part of a play-within-a-play written and performed for their own amusement by characters in the play proper. They intersperse their lines with a good deal of commentary to draw attention to the parallel between Eugenia's situation in *The Bird in a Cage* and Danaë's in the play-within-a-play. The "writer-producer" arranges for offstage music, but no properties, sets, costumes, or other paraphernalia indigenous to masque. The confrontation of Jove and Danaë in the "New Prison" is interrupted by the delivery of a huge cage of birds, which figures prominently in the main plot. The action involving the bird cage is itself spectacular enough to take the place of the obligatory masque sequence.

III *Nondramatic verse*

Most of Shirley's nondramatic verse was published in 1646 as *Poems &c. by James Shirley,* the "&c." referring to commendatory verses, epilogues, prologues, songs from the plays, and all of *The Triumph of Beauty.* Fifty-four newly published poems include complaints, verse epistles, epithalamia, epitaphs, elegies, philosophical dialogues, and a picture poem, "A Catch," featuring die faces. A manuscript collection of Shirley poems in the Bodleian Library at Oxford conains all fifty-four and nine others not printed in the 1646 edition. R. L. Armstrong in his critical edition of Shirley's verse adds ten poems from other manuscript sources.[9] (Two of these ten are only conjecturally Shirley's). Different versions of the same poems in the manuscripts and in the 1646 edition testify to extensive revision over a period of twenty-eight years.

The arrangement, presumably Shirley's, of the poems in the 1646 edition begins and ends with intimate love poems, which flank a group of public poems. The themes of the love poems include *carpe diem* ("Nature no medicine can impart, / When age once snows upon our heart," the last lines of "Cupid's Call"); complaint (of the lover unrequited by a disdainful mistress, as in "To His Unkind Mistress"); praise of the beloved's beauty ("Good Morrow"); constancy ("To his Mistress Confined"); invitation to romance ("Bid me no more good night," in "Good Night"); come-live-with-me ("These are but half the knacks we'll see, and buy, / If you will walk into the fair with me," in "A Fairing"); and love as inspiration ("To L. for a Wreath of Bays Sent"). These poems, like Shirley's plays, reveal his flair for smoothly urbane and witty discourse. A fourteen-line lyric beginning "Would you know what's soft?" answers the question in six octosyllabic couplets (a series of examples of softness), ending with this decasyllabic couplet: "But would you have all these delights in one, / Know but the fair *Odelia*, and 'tis done." The manner is assured, the "delights-Odelia-done" alliteration unobtrusively melodious in an otherwise prosaic sentence with no unusual words (except for the paragon's name), the argument suavely restrained.

"Odelia" appears in several poems, along with Phebe, Daphne, and a number of unnamed mistresses, kind and unkind, all literary sisters of Celia, Lucasta, Althea, and Phillis, idealized beauties addressed by other Caroline poets. Shirley's women here bear a marked resemblance to the heroines of his plays, patterns of beauty and virtue, like the real ladies addressed in the epistles "To the Excellent Pattern of Beauty and Vertue, L.[ady] El.[izabeth] Co.[untess] of Or.[monde]" and "A Letter to the Lady D.[orothy] S.[hirley] sent with a New Comedy." (The name is spelled out in the Dedication of *Changes* to Lady Dorothy Shirley.) Shirley's namesake may or may not have been a distant relative; what is worth noting is that she is titled and that she is characterized as having "authority, and innocence," "vertue," "truth," and "wit," standard attributes of Shirley's heroines.

Although Shirley's poems contain little "information of vital importance," they may "add to our picture of Shirley as a person."[10] At least the image of Shirley the poet to be gained from study of the speakers' personae in his nondramatic verse reveals a sensibility that does not violate the image of Shirley the dramatist that emerges from study of his plays. Shirley's verse, mannered, often facile, sometimes precious, but at its best capturing the essence of the Cavalier mode, belongs to the stylish courtly school of Caroline poetry.

Donne's and Jonson's influences figure prominently in the development of Caroline verse. (The long narrative poem *Narcissus* is unique among Shirley's poems in that this earliest, by all accounts, of his works shows a closer kinship to Shakespeare's *Venus and Adonis* than to any poem written by his later contemporaries.) The cynical speakers and unusual conceits of some of the *Songs and Sonnets* appear occasionally in Carew, Suckling, Cleveland, and

Shirley, while the gentler sound and understatement of Jonson's verse frequently proved to be as congenial to the Cavalier sensibility as Donne's rugged numbers. The Donnean influence on Shirley's verse makes for successful individual poems, but, perhaps surprisingly, not for set pieces in the plays (see Chapter 9). The nondramatic verse of Shirley that suggests Donne's influence includes "To his unkind M.[istris]" ("I will try / From the warm Limbeck of my eye . . . to distil / Tears on thy marble nature"); "Curse" ("Woman, I cannot call thee worse"); and "A Lover that durst not speak to his M.[istris]" ("Thus we may read in spite of standers by, / Whole volumes, in the twinckling of an eye"). Among the complaints one builds on the conceit of a heart turned to stone ("To his unkind M.[istris]"), and another calls a Donnean turn on unrequited love: "couldst thou affection show / To me, I should not love thee so" and "when / Thou art so wise to love again, / Command, and I'll forsake thee then" ("To his Mistris"). Addressing "Fair cruel," the speaker in "To his Mistris upon the Bayes withered" asks for kindness to him instead of praise for his verse. "To the proud mistris" develops a sour-grapes theme. The Jonsonian influence accounts for the classically muted strong emotion of "A Mother hearing her child was sick of the Small-Poxe," "Upon a Gentlewoman that died of a Fever," and the other epitaphs.

More directly concerned with contemporary society and more interested in celebrating great personages, families, houses, and events than Donne, Jonson had a greater influence on Shirley's public poems. Among the best of these, "Upon the Prince's Birth" celebrates the birth of Prince Charles (after the Restoration Charles II) on May 29, 1630, in seven twelve-line stanzas. The lines consist of four, six, eight, or ten syllables. The refrain line ending the first six stanzas, "A joyful sight to see," refers to the bonfires, bell-ringing, and merrymaking of Englishmen, Dutchmen, Frenchmen, Irishmen, Welshmen, Scots, and Spaniards: everyone (except the Puritan) consumes great amounts of liquor. The last stanza is a simple prayer, as light in its way as the lighthearted boisterousness of the preceding stanzas. This buoyant song of praise avoids fulsome compliment by concentrating on joyous reaction to the royal birth. The lightness prevails in spite of the robust activities described because of the alternation of long and short lines that matches the rapid movement from one kind of celebration to another. Shirley's craftsmanship and sound judgment produce a good poem here out of unpromising subject matter.

Shirley's poems have many of the qualities admired by one of his gentlemanly characters, the worthy citizen Goldsworth in *Changes*, who holds his own in a literary discussion with the poetaster Caperwit. Caperwit claims that adjectives "are the flowers, the grace of al our language" and that "with the musicke of / These ravishing Nownes, we charme the silken Tribe, / And make the Gallant melt with apprehension / Of the rare word," while Goldsworth prefers "A row of stately Substantives," a poetic line not "larded" with unnecessary epithets, "ravishing Nownes," or "rare" words, but made up of words that "Carry their weight." "Let children," says Goldsworth, "when they versifie, sticke here, / And there these pidling words for want of matter: / Poets write Masculine numbers" (*Changes, or Love in a Maze*, II.ii). Shirley's best-known poem, "The glories of our blood and state," is written in "Masculine numbers" that not only emphasize "matter" (substantives) with a minimum of decoration ("flowers," adjectives), but also end each line with an accented syllable. Moreover, most of the sentences are simple or compound, with little subordination. The poem develops the old *"sic transit"* theme, a favorite with English poets since Anglo-Saxon times, in firm statement, firm metonymy, firm rhyme, and firm line, long or short. The "rows of stately Substantives" more than "Carry their weight": they give the poem its manly solemnity. "The glories" is justly considered Shirley's best poem.

Shirley's nondramatic verse has intrinsic literary value; it also yields evidence of the same thematic preferences and social orientation as the plays and the masques. It is the work, again, of a competent craftsman capable of occasional poetic flights beyond the bounds of his usually rigidly self-imposed limitations.

CHAPTER 3

"Second Birth":
Plays 1625-1630

SHIRLEY wrote at least five plays between 1626 and 1630, *The Maid's Revenge, The Brothers, The Wedding, The Witty Fair One*, and *The Grateful Servant*.[1] Of these, *The Witty Fair One and The Grateful Servant* reveal clever manipulation of standard theatrical situations and characters, but none of the five fulfills the promise of *Love Tricks*. Shirley's primary responsibility in these years and throughout his career remained a "poem for the scene" that the company he wrote for could stage without too much strain on the players or intellectual challenge to their audiences. The warm reception accorded his efforts indicates the soundness of his judgment. For all its shortcomings, *The Maid's Revenge*, the weakest of the lot, "received encouragement and grace on the *English* Stage," according to the dedication in a 1639 edition. *The Witty Fair One* and *The Grateful Servant*, the best of the five plays, offer interesting enough variations on stock themes; *The Brothers, The Wedding*, and even *The Maid's Revenge* include isolated passages worth noting; but none ventures very far beyond the limits of audience-satisfying entertainment.

I   The Witty Fair One

In this London comedy Sir George Richley, "an old rich Knight," seeks to marry his only heir, Violetta, to Sir Nicholas Treedle, "a Foolish Knight," and tries to ward off the attentions of Aimwell, "a hopefull Gentleman," only moderately well off compared to his rival, who has a considerable fortune as well as a title. The action of the first act takes place in the garden of Sir George's brother Worthy's home, where well-mannered, well-to-do young folk stroll about making light amorous conversation and savoring each other's wit. The play as a whole is made up of several short scenes, with letters and sometimes ghost-written love poems read aloud; eaves-droppers, with soliloquies and asides abounding; and movement on and off stage proceeding at a fast clip. But the quickly spinning world of Shirley's London in *The Witty Fair One* turns on a firm axis, for all the frenetic action moves toward a solidly respectable conclusion.

The setting of the play changes from scene to scene: Worthy's home in London, Treedle's in Croydon, Richley's in London, Aim-well's "lodgings," Fowler's ("a wild young Gentleman"), the street near Richley's house, and the bedchamber of Penelope, Worthy's daughter. Fowler courts the latter, although he denies he loves her: "I hope you wee' not report abroad among my friends," he says to his friend Jack Clare, "that I love her, 'tis the love of mounting into her maydenhead, I vow *Jacke*, and nothing else" (I.iii). The play ends at Worthy's house, where it began, with Fowler ultimately abandoning his rakish ways ("quitting all / Unchast desires" [V.iii]) and speaking the last line of the play, "Nothing is constant but a vertuous mind." The giddy action comes to rest at the home of a worthy gentleman, where love comes to terms with reason.

The dialogue is as rapid as the action and the scene changes. Verbal wit in *The Witty Fair One* ranges from simpleminded word-play to cleverly designed word-picture. Brains, Sir George's servant, helping to "guard" Violetta from unwanted suitors in her father's absence, responds to Clare's "This fellow's mad" with "Nor my Master neither, though he left his braines behind him" (I.iii). Fow-ler's "are you for the Coach" is followed by "Or for the Couch? Take mee a Companion for either" early in his pursuit of Penelope. These two examples are among the less outrageous puns. More sophisti-cated use of language appears in Aimwell's deliberate reconstruction of Violetta's original rejection: "how apt are Lovers to conster (= construe) all to their desires" (a comment by Clare, who had deliv-ered Violetta's message) and in Aimwell's extended description of Treedle, which qualifies as a "character" of a foolish knight.

The most sophisticated language of the play involves the use of Petrarchan terms. Aimwell aims high, Fowler "low," and both use hyperbole to describe their respective would-be lovers, but Fowler undercuts his "Poetical daubings" with "be not you a Goddess I know y'are mortall, and had rather make you my companion than my Idoll." On Violetta's first appearance Aimwell delivers a sonnet-length apostrophe to her charms, beginning "So breakes the day and hides it selfe agen / Among the Westerne shades." Aimwell expresses romantic sentiments straightforwardly, but he acknowledges that "love is but a stragling from our reason." Fowler's praise of Penelope begins "Your hayres are *Cupids* Nets," and in a campaign to break down her defenses he follows his demonstration of mastery of the Petrarchan manner with a commonsense appraisal (like Shakespeare's in Sonnet 130) of his would-be mistress's attributes ("your hand is fine but your gloves whiter"). Fowler's compliments differ from Aimwell's in that they belong to a different order of sensibility, realistic and therefore presumably sane, rather than romantic and therefore mad. But when Fowler protests to his married friend Clare that he enjoys, not loving the ladies, but simply courting them, Clare calls him a "mad lover." In *The Witty Fair One* romantic love, genuine or not, is clearly associated with an unbalanced state of mind.

A silly pair, Treedle and his tutor, provide a comic variation on the love-madness theme. The tutor, who writes "ballads" for "giddy / Chambermaides," dreams of winning Violetta, Treedle's fiancée, with a "Master piece," "Loves hue and cry," duly appropriated by his pupil, whose own literary contribution ("Her foote is feat with Dyamond toes") outdoes the tutor's in fatuity. Because Richley can listen to Treedle's verses without reconsidering the desirability of his daughter's match, even the good old knight's "sanity" and commonsense approach to arranged marriage become suspect.

The irrational behavior to which frustrated lovers, friends, and relatives in *The Witty Fair One* resort takes the form of tricks (Penelope changing places with her maidservant, Fowler pretending to be dying, Violetta outwitting Brains), which occupy the dramatist's major attention in developing his plot and bringing it to a happy conclusion. The occasional farcical incident, especially in the latter acts, punctuates a series of upsetting revelations. Although the machinery of plot complication (misdirected letter, disguise, would-be assignation) has much in common with that of many other seventeenth-century city comedies, Shirley has at least used it cleverly enough here to advance his mild satire of attempts to deal rationally with such irrational matters as love.

The funniest scenes, in which the "dead" Fowler comes to life, appear in the last act. His friends have pronounced him dead, and he cannot persuade the mourners at his wake that he is alive until he announces his "death to vanity, quitting all / Unchast desires" (V.iii) and makes an honorable proposal of marriage to Penelope, which she accepts: "Now you begin to live." The other characters "come to life," too, in ways appropriate to their station in life and individual worth: the marriage of Treedle and Sensible, his ex-fiancée's maid, unites fortune and high social position with good sense; Richley's "consent" to the unauthorized marriage of Aimwell and Violetta shows *his* good sense in recognizing the untitled, relatively "poor" groom's worth. A civilized (sane) society has a proper place for all, the unworthy as well as the worthy, the dull and unprepossessing as well as the witty and the fair. The territory of *The Witty Fair One* may be familiar, but Shirley traverses it with sufficient speed in a freshly enough mounted vehicle to make yet another tour through seventeenth-century city comedy briskly entertaining.

II   The Grateful Servant

The action of *The Grateful Servant* takes place in a royal court, the setting of several of Shirley's plays, whose focal point is most frequently and not surprisingly the reigning prince. The conflict whose resolution it will be the business of the action to pursue, together with the attendant condition of the prince, almost invariably occupies the attention of minor characters, usually two male courtiers, at the beginning of the play. In the opening line of *The Grateful Servant* "The Duke is mov'd," says Giotto to Soranzo (they are "noblemen of Savoy"). Soranzo responds with "The newes displeas'd him much." The news has to do with negotiations for a royal marriage. Further exposition reveals that the Duke's brother, Lodwick, does not sympathize with the Duke's passion for Leonora, their niece, the princess of Milan. Giotto and Soranzo attribute Lodwick's sentiments to his own arranged early marriage. The playwright's purpose in *The Grateful Servant* is to show how love can be reconciled with a state marriage. Leonora is reluctant to marry her uncle, even if such a marriage would keep Milan from becoming subservient to Savoy. The Duke recovers from his disappointment and plans to marry a local girl, whatever her rank. He already has his eye on one Cleona, who lives with Lodwick's neglected wife, Astella.

Leonora in disguise as a page, Dulcino, serves the count Foscari in his suit to win Cleona. Self-sacrificingly, Foscari has Dulcino spread the news that he is dead, so that Cleona will feel free to marry the Duke. Foscari will "looke on" her from "a farre off" (II.ii). He will "die" to Cleona by joining a religious order. Later he confesses his love for her to the Duke: "I / love her above her selfe, and . . . I can give away / Her selfe, Cleona's selfe, in my love to her." The Duke's response is that he "must not be / Oercome in honour" (IV.ii). Foscari and the Duke attempt to outdo each other in noble gestures and in noble language. The characterization of Foscari as a self-sacrificing lover emphasizes his ability to express ever more persuasively his allegiance to ideal love.

Contrapuntal to the progress of Foscari's ascent on the ladder of love is Lodwick's sinking lower and lower into bestiality. But just as Lodwick never reaches the nadir (confronted by the prospect of damnation, he rises above his hellish inclinations), Foscari never quite attains the heights, to which ideal lovers continue to aspire even after they mate.

Shirley might very well have entitled *The Grateful Servant* "The Graceful Servant," whether the term refers to Leonora (as it does) or to Foscari (vis-à-vis Cleona) or to the minor character Belinda (self-styled "servant" to the latent "virtue" of Lodwick). Shirley manipulates his idealized characters and theatrical situations elegantly here. Incidental realism, in the characterizations of the ambitious steward Jacomo and of the equally ambitious courtier Lodwick, counterpoints the exaltation of the noble figures. The "realism" appears in the exposure of preferment and other means of advancement at court. Jacomo and Lodwick provide most of the humorous wit in the play, but no modification of the author's glorification of aristocratic ideals appears to have been intended. The realism of *The Grateful Servant* works to heighten the contrast between the base and the noble. Preoccupation with the latter determines the movement of the action, a balletic movement, a formal, highly stylized, graceful series of gestures designed to evoke an image of honorable struggle to reconcile private inclination with the demands of high social position, struggle that tests the noblest characters' spirit.

The play could well have been conceived as a masque of courtly honor, with the Jacomo and Lodwick scenes constituting an antimasque mocking "the life of greatnesse, and of Court" (Lodwick, III.iv); "They'r fooles that will be frighted from their sport." (The fourth act indeed includes a short masque, involving Lodwick.) For Lodwick position at this point in the play means irresponsible privilege. For the noble lover of Cleona, Foscari, position is not so important as nobility of spirit. Yet he is prepared to forsake the world (enter a monastery) so that Cleona will be free to marry a duke! For both Foscari and the Duke the sacrificial gesture demonstrates the exalted nature of Foscari's refined sentiments. The Duke sees Foscari as a "myracle of honour, and of love" (IV.ii). It is not so much a question, then, of position or of Cleona's happiness—she would be happier as Foscari's wife than as a duchess—as of Foscari's capacity for self-sacrifice to an ideal of love.

If there is another valid explanation of Shirley's characterization of Foscari, it arises from a largely submerged homosexual theme. (The Duke's admission to Leonora in the last scene of the play that "as a boy / I lov'd thee too" is qualified in such a way as to remove any doubt about the nature of that love: "for it could be no other," that is, no other but Leonora.) The theme surfaces in only one direct reference to homosexuality, the Duke's aside in the fourth act, in which he acknowledges to himself the attractiveness of Foscari's page Dulcino:

> My Soul I have examin'd, and yet find
> No reason for my foolish passion
> Our hot *Italian* doth affect these boyes
> For sinne, I've no such flame, and yet methought
> He did appeare most lovely, nay, in's absence
> I cherish his Idea, but I must
> Exclude him, while he hath but soft impression,
> Being remov'd already in his person,
> I lose him with lesse trouble. (IV.ii)

Dulcino's resemblance to a picture of Leonora had troubled the Duke from the first time he saw the page; the Duke had foregone (for "Milan and we are parted" [I.i]) an arranged marriage with a woman he had never seen, but with whom he had fallen in love by "perusing" a picture of her. Most of the other characters in the play mark Dulcino's loveliness with no allusion to the kind of unsettling impression it has on the Duke, as indicated by the aside quoted above. Indeed Foscari warns Dulcino against corruption by court ladies. Yet he is at least as eager to have Dulcino join him in a contemplative life as he is to smooth the way for Cleona's marriage to the Duke: "Tis but a step to heaven, come my sweet boy / Wee climbe by a short ladder to our joy" (IV.iii).

Foscari's ultimate reunion with Cleona receives as short shrift as the Duke-Leonora resolution in a scene dominated by an abbot and several monks. Foscari's transfer from allegiance to God is effected easily and with the abbot's blessing. Much of the last act of *The Grateful Servant* is made up either of the abbot's description of the kind of life monks lead or of the details of Lodwick's reform. The perfunctory treatment given here to the two main pairs of lovers (Lodwick and his long-suffering wife are also reconciled, forming a third pair) suggests that all that Shirley had to say about ideal love had already been said. "Poets shall stretch invention" begins the second-last line of the play. Shirley had already stretched his to its limits in the earlier exclusively "male" Foscari-Dulcino and Foscari-Duke scenes with their lyrical invocations of transcendent love.

III   The Maid's Revenge

The Maid's Revenge is a curious mixture of romantic comedy and revenge tragedy. In the main action Berinthia, younger daughter of a Portuguese gentleman, Gaspar de Vilarezo, will "not be seen" when the Count de Montenegro, "a braggard," and a more worthy suitor, Velasco, come to court her sister Catalina and herself, respectively. Berinthia explains that the older sister must marry first. Both sisters find a third man more attractive than either suitor, their brother Sebastiano's friend Don Antonio de Ribeira. Catalina is upset when she sees him with Berinthia and schemes to get her married to Velasco. Antonio wants his sister, Castabella, to marry Sebastiano. Vilarezo, angry to learn from Velasco that Berinthia has allowed Antonio to court her, commissions Catalina to keep her under lock and key. Discovering a letter Antonio has written Berinthia, Catalina plans to poison her and have Velasco take the blame. These romantic entanglements are untangled ultimately by murder and suicide: Antonio kills Velasco, Sebastiano kills Antonio, Berinthia kills Sebastiano, and Catalina dies of poisoning; Berinthia kills herself, and Castabella retires to a convent.

As a plot outline indicates, nothing in the early part of the play suggests that the action of *The Maid's Revenge* will take a tragic direction. In the first act a rejected suitor does speak of killing a rival, but the threat comes from a comic figure whose ghost-written love sonnets elicit wry criticism—and he is only spurred to further displays of foolishness. Suspicion and jealousy in other characters increase steadily, and it is steadiness that characterizes tragic development here generally, instead of sharp foreboding early on, as in older English tragedy. Consider the openings of some of the best-known Elizabethan and Jacobean tragedies: the chorus in *Faustus*, followed by the protagonist's first soliloquy; Bernardo and Francisco, joined by Horatio and Marcellus, in *Hamlet;* Lodovico's "Banish'd!" in John Webster's *The White Devil;* or Vindice's opening soliloquy in Cyril Tourneur's *The Revenger's Tragedy*. But only the title of *The Maid's Revenge* suggests its tragic direction. In its opening scenes graceful compliment, mild wit, and gentle satire (of a "paper of verses": "They savour of a true Poeticke fury. . . . this line [me] think hath more feet than the rest. . . . here's another lame" [I.ii]) establish a pleasantly urbane atmosphere. The leisurely plotting also helps create the atmosphere of a romantic comedy. The technique works to focus attention on the desirable attributes of high society threatened not by its tolerance of poetasters but by deviations from a strict moral code.

Here and throughout the first two acts, *The Maid's Revenge* points toward a happy ending. The abrupt transition to a tragic tone and the consequent movement toward catastrophe must be judged arbitrary. *The Maid's Revenge* is in reality an aborted romantic comedy. It includes a scene (III.ii) that bears a striking resemblance to the "School of Complement" scene in *Love Tricks*. Ignorant maids and manservants, as well as courtiers, come to a "shirking Doctor's" laboratory for nostrums, gynecological advice, and prognostications. Unlike the "School of Complement" scene in *Love Tricks*, however, the farcical interlude in *The Maid's Revenge* bears no discernible relationship to the play's main action; the connections are some of the characters and the purchase of poison for murder. It is difficult to account for the scene's tonal disturbance without pointing to the Caroline dramatists' practice of interpolating largely irrelevant materials for no other reason than that they entertain.

But the play's most serious flaw is a failure in sensibility, as in a passage from the last act. Sebastiano is warning a new page (Castabella in disguise) that he will be a sad master:

> I am
> Onely in love with sorrow, never merry,
> Weare out the day in telling of sad tales,
> Delight in sighes and teares; sometimes I walke
> To a Wood or River purposely to challenge

> The boldest Eccho, to send backe my groanes
> Ith' height I break e'm. (V.i)

The passage represents the kind of speech some commentators on Caroline drama have considered "attitudinizing," striking a pose, describing an emotion instead of dramatizing it or allowing it to arise out of character and situation. The expression of emotion here is as gratuitous as the violence that ends the play.

IV   The Brothers

In the dedication of *The Brothers* to Thomas Stanley Shirley clearly indicates that he wrote his plays primarily to be staged. He apologizes for this play's appearing "not in that naturall Dress . . . the soul of action." The prologue itself, which was part of the stage production, adopts a disarmingly offhand manner with respect to the play's virtues as a comedy. See it through, Shirley advises his theater audience, and then you can "laugh at the plot, and play." Perhaps we, too, should not take *The Brothers* too seriously. "I / Confess . . . conspiracy," says the actor playing Don Pedro in the epilogue, addressing the audience, "But I am innocent from hurt to you, / And I dare quit the rest [of the actors] from any plot / Meant but to please."

The plot of *The Brothers* traces the way true love overcomes parental disapproval. The characters and situations of city comedy (bourgeois parents' concern with wealth in conflict with their children's with love) appear in *The Brothers* in an upper-middle-class Spanish setting. Francisco and Jacinta love each other, but her father, Don Carlos, disapproves of their marrying because she will be a rich heiress, and Francisco has only a younger brother's fortune to look forward to. Carlos would have Francisco's elder brother Fernando court Jacinta, but he also welcomes Alberto, a friend of his profligate son Luys, as a suitor. Fernando confesses to Francisco that he really loves Felisarda, whose father is the penniless brother of Carlos. Spendthrift Luys tries to persuade his sister to marry Alberto, who promises to support him until he inherits his fortune from Carlos. Carlos overhears Francisco courting Jacinta, and Ferdinand courting Felisarda; the lovers overhear *him* and begin to dissemble for his benefit. Carlos considers a third suitor for Jacinta, Don Pedro de Fuente Calada, and encourages Luys to court Estefania, "a noble Widdow," once Pedro's mistress. Luys has no intention of marrying—Estefania or anyone. Jacinta elopes with Francisco (suddenly a wealthy heir) instead of marrying Pedro. Carlos reminds the disappointed would-be bridegroom of his obligations to Estefania. But when she appears, Pedro renounces her, and she gladly turns to Alberto. The play ends with Pedro and Luys planning to share bachelor quarters.

The Brothers is an attractive play largely because of the characterization of Luys, whose witty speeches in the first two acts have a lusty, rakish quality. The enterprising Luys never runs out of cash to pay for his entertainment. By the end of the second act, for various reasons, and by means of a variety of ingenious ploys, Luys is collecting money from Alberto, Jacinta, his father, and Don Pedro. The last three acts have a different kind of charm, if charm it be, from that of the first two. In the latter part of the play Shirley almost totally abandons Luys's glib chatter for the language of the "religion of love": "female holiness"; "my force / Upon her vowes, can be no less than sacrilege"; "holy contract" (referring not to marriage, but to transcendent mating of souls); "His wife confirm'd by vows, [and] change of hearts" (Francisco's elder brother Fernando and Jacinta have "married" by declaring their eternal love for each other); "his Mistris Armes, / The lovers Sanctuary" (passim, third and fifth acts). And Luys gradually loses his attractiveness, for Shirley transforms him from a roistering rakehell into a sloppy lush. But Luys is back in form at the end of the play when he is gouging money out of Don Carlos with a cock-and-bull story of killing Alberto and running from the police, or beginning a close friendship with his sister's rejected suitor:

Pedro.	Since I cannot have *Jacinta*, I desire
	I may have her brother.
Luys.	Not in marriage.
Pedro.	I like his wit, his spirit, and his humor,
	Do not you love a wench? Luys. Yes sir.
Pedro.	Thou sha't never want. Luys. Wenches?
Pedro.	We'l live together, and if thy Father
	Be not bountifull, thou shalt command my fortune.
Luys.	You speak nobly. (V.iii)

Alas, the play is at an end (except for Pedro's apologies to the brides and Don Ramires's hearty "With Verse and Wine let Poets crown this day"). Whatever new complications may be suggested by the Pedro-Luys exchange remain unexplored.

Admittedly a minor effort, as the author himself makes plain in the prologue and epilogue, *The Brothers* exhibits Shirley's occasional strength in characterization and the weakness in overall structure that marks many of his plays. Not as tonally dissonant as *The Maid's Tragedy*, *The Brothers* nevertheless reveals Shirley's lack of firm control of the play's comic and romantic elements. The transformation of witty, devil-may-care Luys into mindless drunkard constitutes a kind of rake's progress, justifiable enough dramatically if the character did not inexplicably undergo a further transformation into wide-eyed innocent. Similarly, the rationale for the various young lovers' schemes to arrange their own liaisons changes suddenly from affirmation of the superior claims of natural affinity over those of prudence and social status to pseudomystical transcendence of mundane considerations. Yet Francisco and Jacinta engage in comic deception to avoid her marriage to Pedro. Even a "plot / Meant but to please" could benefit from a consistent point of view. Shirley's handling of the more solemn scenes in *The Brothers* bears no trace of irony.

Because *The Brothers* was not published until 1652 (together with five other plays, which Shirley wrote in the early 1640s), it has sometimes been identified with one or another of his lost plays or with an anonymous play, *The Politique Father*.[2] What is interesting is that whether *The Brothers* was written in 1626, when a play by that name was licensed for production, or 1641, its style is as close to that of the early comedies as it is to that of the late. Curiously, *The Brothers* is the only comedy in the 1652 collection, which is otherwise made up of tragedies and tragicomedies. It may be the last comedy Shirley wrote, after *The Constant Maid* in the late 1630s. The choice between 1626 and 1641 as the date of composition cannot be made on the basis of style. A more objective kind of internal evidence, reference to a real or alleged "Spanish plot" of 1641, suggests that the later date is preferable, but by no means certain. To include *The Brothers* among the plays Shirley wrote in the late 1620s violates no theory of his artistic development.

V The Wedding

The Wedding has more than a generic relationship to *The Brothers*. Both plays feature a triple plot, in which young love triumphs

over deception, misunderstanding, or mismatching. In *The Wedding*
Beauford, "a passionate lover," cancels his wedding to Gratiana, an
innocent virgin accused of infidelity, but is ready to marry her by
the end of the play. Marwood, his friend, will marry Lucibel, whose
mother, Cardona, had substituted for Gratiana in Marwood's bed.
Haver, "a yong Gentle-man," and his Jane will marry, leaving the
rejected usurer-suitor Rawbone, "a thin Citizen," alone on stage to
speak the epilogue. In the course of the play Beauford goes through
all the motions of a tragic hero, but escapes the consequences of a
tragic denouement. Marwood rationalizes his "murder" (by "Mili-
sent," Lucibel in disguise as a manservant to Jane) this way: "A live,
as glad to see thee, as thou art / To know thy selfe acquitted for my
death; / Which I of purpose . . . made you beleeve, / T'increase
our joy at meeting" (V.ii). And the Haver-Jane alliance survives
Rawbone's attempt to destroy it. (Her father has only been "testing"
Jane by insisting she marry Rawbone.)

The suspense engendered by all three couples' manufactured
woes depends on such facile stage business as Gratiana's appearance
in a coffin and her father's temporary madness. The "thrills" to be
enjoyed in *The Wedding* are as simpleminded as most of the
"laughs." The play's level of wit can be judged by examining this
exchange between an unlikely suitor of Jane's, Lodam, "a fat Gentleman," and her father:

Lodam.	I can bring her good qualities, if she want any: I have travail'd for em.
Landry.	What are they?
Lodam.	The Languages.
Landry.	You suspect shee will want tongue:—let me see—Parlez Fran-zois monsieur.
Lodam.	Diggon a camrag. [= digon a Cymraig, "enough of Welsh"³]
Landry.	That's Welsh.
Lodam.	Pocas palabras. [= "a few words"]
Landry.	That's Spanish.
Lodam.	Troth I have such a confusion of languages in my head, you must e'en take em as they come.
Landry.	You may speake that more exactly—Havelar spagniol, Sig-nior?
Lodam.	Serge-dubois,—Calli-mancho, et Perpetu-ana. [names of "stuffs," various kinds of cloth]

Landry.   There's stuffe, indeede, since you are so perfect, Ile trust you
                for the rest. I must referre you sir unto my daughter, if you
                can winne her faire opinion, my consent [may] happily follow.
                (III. ii)

The humor here exploits an insular audience's fear and distrust of
foreigners and of foreign travel for Englishmen; their contempt for
too much learning (which has succeeded only in confusing Lodam);
their gratification at the spectacle of an Englishman affecting poly-
lingualism; and their delight in garbled foreign tongues, as much
a source of fun on stage as accented English. Shirley might well
have foregone his apologia for *The Brothers*, inventive and imaginative as it is in much of the characterization of Luys, and reserved
it for *The Wedding*, which offers no such relief from its turgid rehash
of stage clichés. "It hath passed the Stage," writes Shirley in the
dedication, and, not content with his success there, offers it to a
patron he considers a worthy judge of "excellency in the Musicall
Arte of Poesie," from whom he does not doubt "it shall receive a
kinde welcome."

    The Wedding has received an unwarranted amount of scholarly
attention, and for dubious reasons. Alfred Harbage, for example,
grouped *The Wedding* with "the sophisticated comedies, *The Ball*,
Hyde Park, *The Gamester*, and *The Lady of Pleasure*, wherein Shirley anticipated Restoration playwrights by drawing his materials,
dangerously sometimes, from contemporary life in fashionable cir-
cles."[4] But the extent to which Shirley based the characters in these
plays on Londoners of his time cannot be determined with any
degree of accuracy. Nor does *The Wedding's* mindless romanticism
prefigure the sometimes abrasive realism of Restoration comedy.
The characters in *The Wedding* are uncomplicated theatrical types.
The fools have no "redeeming qualities," the heroes and heroines
subscribe to conventional ideals of honor without question, and the
villains are simply villainous. Shirley's best city comedies, *Hyde
Park* and *The Lady of Pleasure*, manipulate with greater subtlety
and sophistication the conventions of the genre to which *The Wedding* belongs.

CHAPTER 4

"A Ripe Young Man":
Plays 1631-1632

L ONDON theaters were closed for six months in 1630 because
of the plague. Soon after they reopened, toward the end of the
year, new plays by Shirley began to appear in quick succession. In
1631 and 1632 the Queen's men produced six of them, *The Traitor*,[1]
Love's Cruelty, The Humourous Courtier,[2] *Changes, Hyde Park*,
and *The Ball*,[3] plays of varying degrees of quality individually, but
together an impressive group, more than adequate testimony to
Shirley's having arrived at maturity as a dramatist.

The world of the first three plays is a ducal court, a world of
"preferments, honours, offices" (*The Traitor*, II.i). As such it is
despotic only from the point of view of envious outsiders who have
tried and failed to gain entrance there themselves, or of insiders
envious of the prince's favorites. In or out of favor with royalty,
Shirley himself seems never to have questioned the legitimacy,
indeed the divine rightness, of the institution, although some
princely characters in his plays use their power unwisely. From
Shirley's point of view King Charles I was entirely within his rights
when he defied Parliament and proclaimed Personal Rule in 1629.
The tragicomedy *The Grateful Servant* of that year had already
recorded the ambitious outsider's distorted concept of privilege:
"mee thinkes I talke, like a peremptorie Statesman already, I shall
quickly learne to forget my selfe, when I am in great office, I will
oppresse the Subject, flatter the Prince, take bribes a both sides,
do right to neyther, serve Heaven as farre as my profit will give me
leave, and tremble, only at the Summons of a Parliament" (Jacomo,
II.i). None of the characters in *The Traitor, Love's Cruelty*, or *The
Humourous Courtier* "trembles" at any summons except the Duke's:
"Princes are dangerous and carry death / Upon their tongue" (Bel-

lamente in *Love's Cruelty*, I.ii); "Princes are gods on earth" (Eubella, II.ii); "Princes loose their awe that are too mild" (the Duke himself, III.iv). Tragedy in *Love's Cruelty* and in *The Traitor*, however, arises not from the authoritarianism of a prince, but from intellectual curiosity and conflicting loyalties, respectively. Both plays are primarily tragedies of love, with revenge figuring secondarily in *The Traitor*, in spite of its title.

The world of *Changes*, *Hyde Park*, and *The Ball* is contemporary London, a "community / Of fooles and wisemen" (*Changes*, IV.iii), as in *Love Tricks*. The promise of Shirley's first play is finally fulfilled in *Hyde Park*, the best of the four comedies among the six plays. The better of the two tragedies is *Love's Cruelty*, a quite distinctive achievement among Shirley's tragedies and tragicomedies.

I Love's Cruelty

Love's Cruelty presents an apparently irresistible movement toward adultery and death. The instigator of the action, witty and willful Clariana, makes a dying gesture toward conventional morality ("Oh wives, hereafter, meane your hearts to them / You give your holy vowes" [V.ii]), but the action of the play insists on the tyranny of the sexual instinct; "holy vowes" cannot protect the victims of love's cruelty. And even more important, the design of the action insists on the inescapability of sin, given the natural human desire for forbidden knowledge.

When Clariana and Bellamente first declare their mutual love, she discovers that his best friend, Hippolito, refuses to meet her, for "he dares not trust / His frailty with thy sight" (Bellamente to Clariana, I.i), at least until she is married. Clariana, without revealing her identity, arranges a meeting with Hippolito to satisfy her curiosity about such a "strange friend." Later Bellamente finds her in a compromising situation, but she is able to persuade him of Hippolito's ignorance and of her own innocent motives. Soon after Bellamente and Clariana marry, he finds her in bed with Hippolito. "Tel me *Clariana*," he asks her, "how couldst thou / Use me so cruelly?" (IV.i). They will continue to live together, but only for appearance's sake. A final encounter between Clariana and Hippolito on his wedding day ends with their stabbing each other; Bellamente commits suicide. Clariana is clearly responsible for what happens, but it is not so much that she is evil as that the sexual instinct is despotic.

Recognition of the power of sexual instinct makes the Duke of Ferrara tolerant of the promiscuity of courtiers Bovaldo and Hippolito. The Duke himself sets a poor example by trying to enlist virtuous Eubella's father Sebastian and putative lover Hippolito in his pursuit of her. Although less exalted go-betweens (pages, grooms, and maids) figure only incidentally as part of the background, which includes taverns and whorehouses, they help create a threatening ambience of sexual tension and release.

Love's Cruelty is relatively free of the complicated intrigues and plots that clutter many of Shirley's plays. The main action (Clariana-Bellamente-Hippolito) alternates scene by scene with the Duke-Eubella-Sebastian action. The symmetry of the alternation polarizes attitudes toward sexual promiscuity. Most of the play is made up of polite arguments, even at its emotional climaxes, where rigid moral positions are successively modified until the final tragic outburst. The reform of the Duke (he now intends to marry Eubella) reinforces the traditional standard of morality: the wittiness of Clariana, Hippolito, and Bovaldo becomes sophistry in retrospect. The largely passive, constantly moralizing Eubella is the model of virtuous courtly behavior. The neatness of the play's structure may obscure its unique claim to distinction as a parable of the dangers of intellectual curiosity. Not sexuality draws Clariana into a relationship that develops into a fatal sexual liaison, but interest in discovering the psychological basis for Hippolito's diffidence about meeting his best friend's fiancée. Is it the pose of an insufferable *précieux*? Can such a paragon of friendship be genuine? Can human emotion survive on such a rarefied plane? The Duke and Eubella reconcile sexuality and morality; theirs is a socially acceptable solution to the long-drawn-out campaign of the Duke to corrupt her. What happens to Clariana and Hippolito is the wages of sin, the sin of Eve and Adam.

Shirley's ladies and gentlemen in *Love's Cruelty* zestfully flourish their banners of sexual liberation (which used to be called libertinism). As she lies in bed with her husband's best friend, Clariana sings snatches of a lusty ballad between polished arguments that forbidden fruit is the sweetest (IV.i). Shirley is seemingly equally playful, but not as oblivious to the consequences of his playfulness, in arranging the construction of *Love's Cruelty*, which veers toward romantic comedy, then tragicomedy, but suddenly stumbles into a bloody resolution. The guilty lovers kill each other, not without "High and prevailing oratory, to / Express what my heart labours with!" (V.ii), for which Clariana yearns in the play's last scene. She dies with these words: "Thy sword was gentle to me, search't againe, / And thou shalt see / How my embracing blood Will keepe it warme / And kisse the kind destroyer." For the first time Shirley's verse penetrates beyond its usually secure limitations, more than justifying the liberties he took with traditional dramatic modes.

After *Love's Cruelty* Shirley did not attempt tragedy again until 1639 (if *The Politician* can rightly be called a tragedy). He never wrote another tragedy like *Love's Cruelty*, or any play as experimental with dramatic form as this unique creation was. Shirley's forte was comedy, and the four plays immediately following *Love's Cruelty* include one, *The Humourous Courtier*, that belongs among his more pedestrian efforts, and one, *Hyde Park*, that ranks among his best in whatever genre.

II Hyde Park

Shirley's greatest achievement in *Hyde Park* is his handling of the plot involving Carol and Fairfield, easily as charming a pair of reluctant lovers as Beatrice and Benedick or Millamant and Mirabel. After an opening scene in which Lacy, eager to marry Bonavent's rich "Widdow," deplores the influence of the "coy Lady that lives with her" (Carol, her cousin-in-law) to the point where he says "tis pittie any place / But a cold Nunnery should be troubled with her" (I.i), Carol first appears to be as indifferent to love as Lacy thinks she is. But Carol is not cold; she wishes Mrs. Bonavent were not so easy to wed: "We Maides are thought the worse on, for your easiness" (I.ii). *Talk* of love, the language of courtship, bores Carol: "is any thing more ridiculous?" she asks Fairfield in their first scene together. But they both thrive on *witty* talk, on any subject. Like Beatrice and Benedick in Shakespeare's *Much Ado About Nothing*, they pick up words and phrases from each other's speeches in a game of verbal one-upmanship. Besides compliments Carol dislikes presents and pleas "to waite upon" a lady. She wins the first round of this battle of the sexes with Fairfield.

The second round is a tie, with the edge Fairfield's. He promises not to court her if she will swear to grant him a single request before she knows it, but only after he has agreed to whatever "exceptions" to the request she stipulates. The request is that she is not to love him or desire his company. In the third round Fairfield appears to be interested in another woman (actually his sister, Julietta). The

setting is the park, and the lovers see, but do not speak to, each
other. By now Carol must tell herself, "keepe in, great heart" (III.i).
So the third round is Fairfield's. The fourth is Carol's; Fairfield, out
to "humble" her, winds up hanging on the ropes. Thinking she loves
him, he releases her from her oath. Carol pretends not to care,
delivering a low blow. "I am an Infidell to use him thus" (III.ii),
she declares in an aside. Fairfield is as discomfited as Jane Austen's
Darcy when Elizabeth turns him down in *Pride and Prejudice*. Carol
wins the round—but the third act ends with her admitting to herself
that she may have gone too far: "I must to th' coach and weepe, my
heart will break else, / I'me glad he does not see me." Each holds
his own in the company of others in the fourth act, where Carol
learns that Julietta is Fairfield's sister. In the last act two well-
matched champions meet and are ready to mate on equal terms:

Carol.	Say ist a Match? speak quickely, or for ever
	Hereafter hold your peace.
Fairfield.	Done!
Carol.	Why done!
Fairfield.	Seale and deliver.
Carol.	My hand and heart, this shall suffice till morning.
Fairfield.	Each others now by conquest, come let's to e'm.
	If you should false [fail?] now
Carol.	Hold me not worth the hanging. (V.i)

The battle of the sexes in *Hyde Park* marks a high point in Shirley's
theatrical craftsmanship, for the Carol-Fairfield action develops
within the rules of a game whose tenuousness Shirley perhaps acknowledges when he has Carol ask Fairfield, rhetorically, during
a brief impasse: "Be you no prompter, to insinuate / The first word
of your studied Oration?" (III.ii). The studied nature of the spon-
taneity in the Carol-Fairfield scenes detracts not a whit from their
attractiveness.

With *Hyde Park* Shirley achieved both success on the stage (in
the dedication he speaks of the "Applause it once receiv'd in the
action") and literary distinction, not least in the manipulation of the
verse, although that is not usually cited as a distinct asset to the
play. The sophisticated verse of *Love's Cruelty* probed the very
assumptions on which poetic expression rests and in the process
revealed the potentially dangerous tentativeness of the conventions
Shirley works with so cavalierly in the play. The verse of *Hyde Park*
is of a different order, not so much evocative as workmanlike in its

versatility, and serves a different purpose, not to explore the vulnerability of convention, but to reinforce the concept of the viability of traditional form. Ironically, scholarly discussion of *Hyde Park* usually includes some statement about the play as a precursor of Restoration comedy and therefore as innovative.[4] True, the blank verse line is well adapted to the dialogue of *Hyde Park*'s urbane characters, but there is no indication of dissatisfaction with it. Restoration dramatists abandoned verse frequently for prose, which in their best works aspires to the condition of poetry. The opening lines of *Hyde Park* move confidently back and forth between conversational half-lines and more carefully measured full ones, indicating not an inclination toward the condition of prose, but a sense of the immediate heightening of expression possible even within conversation that dramatic verse can produce:

Trier.	And how and how?
Lacy.	The cause depends.
Trier.	No Mistress.
Lacy.	Yes, but no Wife.
Trier.	For now she is a Widdow.
Lacy.	But I resolve—
Trier.	What does she say to thee.
Lacy.	Shee sayes, I know not what she sayes, but I must take another course, and yet she is—
Trier.	A creature of much sweetenesse, if all tongues Be just in her report, and yet tis strange Having seven years expected, and so much Remonstrance of her Husband's losse at Sea, She should continue thus.
Lacy.	What if she should Renew the bond of her devotion For seven yeares more.
Trier.	You will have time enough, To pay in your affection. (I.i)

Like the verse, the action of *Hyde Park* combines formality and informality as Shirley celebrates an ideal of social life, based on the prevailing mores of Londoners in the 1630s. All ten major characters, including a nobleman, observe the rules of courtesy while they go about the business of making love and having fun. Lord Bonvile is described as having a "Noble Nature, valiant, bountiful" and a "spirit equall to his fortunes." That is, he is very active sexually: he is also described as a "gentleman that loves cleane Napery," who, "next

to a Woman . . . loves a running horse" (I.i). "Cleane Napery" is
a euphemism for a "lady of pleasure," and Bonvile bets on horse
races. But whether gambling or attempting to seduce Julietta, Bonvile conducts himself like a gentleman. The concluding line of the
first scene, "Lets walke, and thinke how to behave our selves,"
could serve as an epigraph for the play as a whole.

Manners are politely urbane. The disguised Bonavent, curious
but not anxious about his wife's fidelity, asks Carol about Mistress
Bonavent's marriage to Lacy: "I heare that gentlewoman's married"
(III.i). When Carol responds affirmatively, Bonavent ventures a
direct, but delicately phrased, inquiry into the possibility of a pren-
ruptial affair ("Dee think he has bin aforehand") and launches an
amusing, simple, but not insensitive play on words involving cards:
"In English has he plaid the forward gamester, / And turnd up
trump." Carol accepts the challenge: "Before the cards be Shuffled? /
I lay my life you meane a coate Card. / Deale againe, you gave one
to many / In the last tricke, yet Ile tell thee what I thinke." And what
she thinks is that Mistress Bonavent "and you might ha showne
more wit. . . . She to ha kept her selfe a Widdow, and / You not
to have asked me such a foolish question." The exchange is spirited,
but not heated; sophisticated, but far from superficial. Good manners combined with lively wit accommodate potentially offensive
subjects of converstion.

In almost every scene the wit flirts with bawdiness, acknowledging
sexual curiosity without suggesting prurience. Salty remarks such
as "to give her a heate this morning" (referring to a gentleman
summoned by the supposed widow of the supposedly lost merchant
Bonavent) by Trier, Lacy, Venture, and Rider, the lusty bachelors
whose dialgoue opens the play, appear in their speech alongside
expressions such as "Renew the bond of her devotion" (referring to
an extension of the seven-year-old waiting period for a wife whose
husband may have been lost at sea) that attest to the existence of
personal and social commitments in a larger area of concern than
sex. And of course the young men are ready to duel at the drop of
an imagined insult or if a "Mistresse love and honour" are involved.

The ladies are equally saucy—and equally observant of a code of
behavior appropriate to their class. At Hyde Park, where men as
well as horses run races, Carol asks Mistress Bonavent, "Cousen,
do they run naked?" (III.i). "That were a most immodest sight,"
replies Mistress Bonavent. Carol persists: "Here have bin such fel-
lowes, Cousen." And when her cousin says the spectacle "would

fright the women," Carol points out that "Some are of opinion it brings us hither." Mistress Bonavent's prudence never descends into prudery, and Carol's candor never suggests disingenuousness, for she is consistently frank. She might, indeed, be representing at its best the high life of London in Shirley's time, as it sometimes hovers precariously on the edge of looseness, but most often maintains a firm balance between currently fashionable mores (including strictures regarding subjects fit for conversation among ladies) and mature, independent judgment.

Carol's manner features a unique form of verbal wit. While she and Fairfield carry on their exchanges with some asperity, the other couples more often deal in the hyperbole of romantic courtship ("I should be surfeted with happiness" [II.iii]), allowing for a rather gentler wordplay ("Surfets in the Spring / Are dangerous"). Julietta, actively involved in the romantic activities of her milieu, articulates its moral code most clearly and most consistently ("he that's truely noble will not staine his honor" and "Can love degenerate in noble breasts" [III.i]). Romantic courtship, odious to Carol (a "nimble lady," that is, a lady with an active mind), detracts from "the Noblenesse of . . . birth and nature" in her suitor, who, she says, should keep his "priviledge," his "Masculine property" (I.ii). This young lady clearly has a mind of her own.

Carol belongs to the same social class as her cousin. Mistress Bonavent as a woman of means has "liberty . . . servants . . . Jeweles . . . a Coach . . . a Christian Livery . . . a waitingwoman . . . [pets] . . . pretty Wardrobe . . . Tayler of [her] owne . . . a Doctor" (I.ii). She is free to talk "loud and idle at [her] table," to sing a "wanton ditty," to "Dance and goe late to bed." That Mistress Bonavent avails herself only temperately of these privileges seems likely, since she appears most frequently to be more concerned with discharging her duties as widow, fiancée, newlywed bride, wife, and hostess. At her wedding party she apologizes to the stranger (her "lost" first husband in disguise) for her new husband's forcing him to dance: "Pray impute it / No trespasse studdied to affront you Sir, / But to the merry passion of a Bridegroome" (II.ii). To put an uninvited guest, a stranger, at ease obviously involves more than tact and etiquette: Bonavent's appearance, even in disguise, indicates that he belongs to Mistress Bonavent's world. Earlier, her servant offered him wine—because he looked like a gentleman. With a member of the nobility, such as Lord Bonvile, courtesy extends beyond hospitality to special concerns: in the last act Lacy,

Mistress Bonavent's new husband (of less than a full day) proposes music and dancing for His Lordship's entertainment (less vigorously than for Bonavent in the second act, to be sure). Deference to nobility and even to the appearance of gentility stops short of equating respectability with position or ancestry, while the taste for wit and dalliance in Carol and Mistress Bonavent's circle does not mean tolerance of impropriety.

In the third and fourth acts Shirley exploits the Hyde Park setting to evoke a compelling image of civilized recreation. Elegant ladies and gentlemen stroll leisurely through the park in the springtime, laughing lightly, stopping to listen to a nightingale—or a cuckoo— heading for the lodge to drink a "sillabub," raising the question of an assignation as casually as that of a gambling loss. Some gentlemen alone may be spying (for plot purposes), but do so discreetly: "two'not / Be indiscretion to observe him" (IV.iii). Others contemplate their chances at the races in livelier terms (Venture, a gentleman jockey: "He must be a Pegasus that beates me" [IV.iii]) and find the park an excellent setting for a ballad about outstanding thoroughbreds (Lord Bonvile: "does any tune become / A gentleman so well as a ballad"). Venture sings of "wellbreath'd Jilian Thrust." The ladies stop to drink each other's healths with fresh milk and to banter with a smart young page. Fairfield kisses a pretty milkmaid just before offstage noises of betting and racing begin. Carol "ventures" silk stockings against Julietta's perfumed gloves on Venture's race. A bagpiper plays a galliard for Bonavent after the race. Shirley throughout the two acts has not only sustained an urban-pastoral dynamic, but has also assimilated incidental sexual innuendo and a climactic near-duel (politely averted by the would-be combatants, without dishonor to either). The scenes in Hyde Park glow with good humor, good manners, and good sense. In a parenthesis in the concluding act Carol notes that "Poets write enough of hell"; in Hyde Park Shirley has created a kind of heaven-on-earth for privileged Londoners of the 1630s, "a vicious age," according to no less an authority than Julietta.

The Hyde Park scenes end with gamekeepers praising the nobility of Bonvile, who has tipped them lavishly. The ambience of the park is easy, pleasant, relaxed, celebrating the way of life of mostly youthful members of a leisure class. But the idyllic scene remains essentially dramatic, for the Carol-Fairfield, Julietta-Bonvile, and Bonavent-Mistress Bonavent-Lacy actions advance there toward resolution.

It is just that the setting is characterized as vividly as the dramatis personae.

All the action of *Hyde Park* takes place on a single day, the third and fourth acts within Hyde Park itself.[5] The day is the last in a seven-year waiting period for an apparent widow, Mistress Bonavent, who remarries but does not consummate the marriage because her long-lost husband returns. The Bonavent plot, no more prominent than two other man-woman plots, is subordinated like them to the overall tribute to gracious living described above.[6] The outcome of each plot testifies to a basically sound social structure, celebrated with affection as Shirley depicts the amorous pursuits of privileged Londoners who will perpetuate an urbane community's charming way of life. Most of them are witty, some are wise, and those who gamble on love and marriage as they might on horse races suffer no greater disappointment than they would if they had made a foolish bet at the track.[7] In other plays Shirley's satire of fools bites more harshly; here, even "underlings," also elsewhere in Shirley's plays characterized with a measure of scorn, receive gentle treatment. A milkmaid serving syllabub, a soft-spoken young waiting-woman, and a cheeky fifteen-year-old page make brief but telling appearances as minor figures in the background of a landscape dominated by nobler souls. The entire cast of characters present together a good-humored image of a world as attractive and as unreal as Margaret Mitchell's antebellum Tara.

Setting and contemporaneity notwithstanding, *Hyde Park* limits realism to innocuous reference to well-known taverns, gardens, and bowling alleys; races at Newmarket; Bedlam; the New Exchange in the Strand; and the famous park itself. A few graphic anatomical and sexual references, which Victorian commentators on the play considered coarse, but which literary naturalists might consider fundamental, are absorbed by the sophisticated dialogue. Although Shirley does not idealize the leading characters, they exhibit a great affinity to idealized types and little of the individual complexity associated with psychological realism. The action itself depends upon such tried-and-true theatrical devices as forged letters and "testing" of lovers' faithfulness. Yet the created world of *Hyde Park* has a distinctive momentum and a self-propelled direction and purpose that produce artistic consistency even if they do not mirror historical realities.

The *raison d'être* of the play, to provide a London entertainment for Londoners, does not preclude attention to its function as dramatic

vehicle of moral enlightenment—indeed, it unquestioningly involves such consideration from Shirley's point of view. Yet explicitly
moralistic passages do not figure prominently until the last act, are
largely confined to the Julietta-Bonvile-Trier triangle, and even
there are smoothly integrated into the dramatized rationale for a
young lady's choosing a chastened would-be seducer (Bonvile) over
the suitor (Trier) who tested her virtue by describing her secretly
to Bonvile as a "lady of pleasure." Certainly these speeches of Julietta
do not disfigure her characterization (as similar ones do that of Albina
in *The Politician*, limited as they are to articulation of abstract morality). Shirley paid his dramatic dues to Julietta in the first four acts
and earned the right to have her preach a little in the last.

The fidelity with which Shirley reproduces in *Hyde Park* so much
of the London life of his time does not make the play realistic, and
it should not suggest that any of the characters have real-life counterparts. In a play like *Hyde Park* such a suggestion would probably
be harmless, but in a play like *The Ball* it could—and did—cause
trouble for the dramatist.

III   The Ball

In Shirley's time government censorship frequently inhibited
production of stage plays for alleged satire of prominent public figures. Sir Henry Herbert, the "Master of the Revels" to whom producers submitted play scripts for endorsement, has an entry for
November 18, 1632, in his office-book indicating approval with conditions of production of Shirley's *The Ball*. Christopher Beeston,
manager of the acting company known as Queen Henrietta's men,
was to delete offensive passages, those in which "ther were divers
personated so naturally, both of lords and others of the court, that
I took it ill, and would have forbidden the play, but that Biston
promiste many things which I found faulte withall should be left
out, and that he would not suffer it to be done by the poett any
more, who deserves to be punisht. . . ."[8] Since Herbert found fault
with "many things" in *The Ball*, these were probably deleted early
in production and long before publication in 1639. The play in its
extant form still makes its point clearly enough about one of the
"vulgar errors" of Shirley's day. Many Londoners apparently believed that the new subscription balls promoted promiscuity. *The
Ball* tries to set the record straight.

Lord Rainbow, a "ladies' idol" (so described by his friend Colonel
Winfield), is "a great advancer / Of the new Ball" (I.i). Such an association made at the first mention of a ball in the play hints at just
the sort of amorous sport its detractors think goes on there. When
two young ladies, Lady Rosamond and Lady Honoria, interested
romantically in Lord Rainbow, vie with each other in claiming precedence in his affections, reference to the ball suggests assignation.

Rosamond.   I have
              I must confesse discourst of his good parts,
              Desir'd his company.
Honoria.   And had it?
Rosamond.   Yes, and had it.
Honoria.   All night.
Rosamond.   You are not I hope jealous,
              If I should say all night I neede not blush,
              It was but at a Ball; but what of this? (I.ii)

In preparation for Lord Rainbow's ball Lady Rosamond and Lady
Honoria take dancing lessons with Lady Lucina, "a young rich
widow" courted by four suitors. One of these, Winfield, comes to
Lucina's defense when they discover how she has been making fun
of all four. The three rejected suitors, Lamount, Travers, and Bos-
tock, complain to Rainbow, who appears to promise "satisfaction"
for their grievances at the ball (IV.i).

Winfield is Lucina's choice if he can swear he has never had a
woman. The worthy thirty-year-old colonel says he cannot lie; nor
does he expect her to have been "honest" before she met him. He
sets a single standard for both and accepts her attendance at balls
as evidence of her own indulgence in sexual adventures. Lucina
responds: "The world imagines so" (IV.iii). Once they are engaged
to marry, she is ready to make him see that what the "world imagines" is not so. Winfield goes to the ball, although he no longer
needs proof of its innocence.

The last act takes place in the Ball Room, where a masque begins
with the descent of a golden ball to Venus, Cupid, and Diana. Cupid
disdains his mother and awards the ball to Diana, who accepts it
and leaves with him, for "Love is welcome while he's chast" (V.i).
Everybody at the ball can now see that it is not a gathering-place
for debauchery—everybody but a disgruntled suitor of Honoria, the
railer-cynic Barker, who threatens to malign the ball. But malice
is not alone the reason for the ball's scandalous reputation. Those

ignorant of the truth may suspect that where there's smoke, there's fire, just as Lady Lucina and Colonel Winfield in their ignorance of each other's true nature assumed, respectively, that a soldier must needs be an experienced lover and that a fashionable London lady who attends balls must be promiscuous.[9]

The didactic intent of *The Ball* is clear enough; unfortunately, so is its exploitation of scandal. The titillation afforded by rumors of scandal persists until the last act, where they are exposed as false: the sequence has the effect of a reverse striptease. Several years after its original production, *The Ball* was published without a dedication or prologue, while Shirley was in Ireland. Listed among his publications in a 1653 collection of his plays as *The Ball*, or *French Dancing Master* (referring to a minor comic character, M. le Frisk, who speaks French-accented English), the play belongs in the Shirley canon even if he would not have approved of its publication in its extant form (the 1639 edition). Perhaps Herbert's censorship eliminated scenes that integrated the disparate parts of the play as we know it.

IV   Changes, or Love in a Maze

This city comedy rings few new changes on generic characters and situations. Nubile maidens, courting lovers, concerned elders, and a motley crew of arrivistes, poetasters, and underlings proceed through a series of misunderstandings and mistaken identities to happy resolutions of problems for all except fools who cannot change. The single plot variation has a young man frankly admitting his love for twins, both of whom love him.

Sir John Woodhamore, uncle of Eugenia, and Goldsmith, father of Chrysolina and Aurelia, open the play with a discussion of suitors (Yongrave and Gerard) for the girls. Sir Gervase Simple, a now-impoverished country gentleman who bought his knighthood, has come to town with his son Thump to marry one of Goldsmith's daughers, neither of whom he has met. Goldsworth does not encourage him, but his wife, who "affects this Knight / For's title" (I.ii), does. Chrysolina and Aurelia admit to Goldsworth that they love Gerard, and Gerard tells him he loves them both. The sisters agree to let Gerard choose between them. He means to have his friend Frank Thornay choose one twin for himself; Gerard will gladly take the other. Thornay appears to be choosing Chrysolina, who refuses his suit. He suggests to Gerard that he deliberately ignore her, so that Aurelia may feel free to marry him. Gerard proceeds to scorn Chrysolina and declare himself to Aurelia. Chrysolina pretends to love Thornay, but when Yongrave tells her that Thornay is betrothed to Eugenia, she spurns any further suit. Aurelia spurns Gerard for spurning Chrysolina, who now finds herself falling in love with Yongrave.

Thornay now regrets his suit of Aurelia and neglect of Eugenia. Yongrave retreats when he learns that Thornay really loves Eugenia. In the last act Eugenia and Thornay are reconciled, as are Yongrave and Chrysolina, and Gerard and Aurelia. The maze these lovers create for themselves by constantly changing partners leads them into a dead end of mismatching until they find a way out by revealing their true feelings and honorable intentions. The three pairs of legitimate lovers and a fourth of Simple and "Lady Bird" (a page disguised as a beautiful young woman) appear at the end of the play in a masque whose action reveals to the rest of the characters the solutions that the lovers in a maze already found to their problems. A youthfully exaggerated sense of honor caused their changes in affection and allegiance; common sense dispels their doubts and fears.

Although the main features of this comedy add little to what Shirley had already accomplished in the genre, *Changes* has an unmistakable charm. It owes its attractiveness to the disarming perspective on the main action provided by a self-consciousness about his craft that Shirley usually reserves for dedications and prologues. Incidental discussion of poets and poetry includes Goldsworth's strictures regarding "Masculine numbers," emphasizing common sense and substance ("Substantives") without unnecessary frills: the complications of the main plot are unraveled when the romantic young couples learn to speak their minds plainly.

There is no lack of pretty verse in *Changes*, but the attitude toward it is consistently skeptical. After a particularly flowery address by Gerard, Aurelia says, "I must confesse you have exprest a Lover, / Wanted no Art to flourish your warme passion: / But language is no clew to guide us to / The knowledge of your heart (III.iii). Another of the girls courted in the play lets a prospective lover know immediately

> I doe not love set speeches nor long praises,
> I hope y'ave made no verses o' my haire,
> Acrosticks o' my name, I hate them worse

Than witchcraft, or the place I live in: if
You be a sutor, put me out of my paine,
Quickly I beseech you. (Eugenia to Yongrave, II.i)

Elsewhere in the play Shirley lightly satirizes pretensions in verse
and in untalented versifiers. The poetaster Caperwit's greeting to
a young lady that parodies Romeo ("Thus breakes *Aurora* from the
Easterne hills, / And chaseth night away" [I.ii]) provokes mockery,
but Caperwit persists undaunted. His estimation of a rival suitor
depends upon degree of poetic fury: "How many raptures does he
talke a day? / Is he transported with Poeticke rage? / When was he
stil'd Imperiall wit?" "Who loves not verse is damn'd," says Caperwit. With difficulty Simple composes a few verses, which he delivers with his eyes shut, holding the hand, he thinks, of his beloved,
and kissing "her" before he opens them, only to find he has em-
braced his rival. Poetasters face the truth of their absurdity but are
too foolish to change.

Among the more pleasant aspects of the comedy in *Changes* is
the wit of all three heroines. It is not yet so waspish as that of
Restoration heroines, but still quite tart, as when it is dealing with
ardent suitors armed with fashionable verse: Eugenia's request to
Yongrave is a good example. Not surprisingly, it is a nonpoet, a man
characterized as worthy and cultivated, with a taste for reading good
verse, who advises the poetaster how to write well—with a minimum
of adjectives: "Masculine numbers" feature more "Substantives"
(Goldsworth to Caperwit [II.ii]). Authentic speech in Shirley's plays
is indeed written in "Masculine numbers"; inept or pretentious
speech, full of unnecessary epithets, marks the would-be gentleman
in *Changes*, (Simple), the ambitious bourgeoise (Mistress Goldsworth), and the poetaster (Caperwit).

The good-natured tone of *Changes* lightens the satire of its easy
targets. Shirley is having fun with Mistress Goldsworth, Simple,
and Caperwit, but it is amiable, affectionate fun. In fact, he adopts
an easygoing attitude toward all the materials he is working with in
Changes, content for the most part with a reshuffling of stock figures
and complications. Some freshening of the poetaster cliché can be
detected in the characterization of Caperwit (who describes the
popularity of gratuitous spectacle on stage with some insight into
its essential triviality; let it not be forgotten that *Changes* itself, as
a comedy of its time de rigeur ends with a masque), but none in
that of the freshly minted knight from the country. *Changes* is the

work of a competent craftsman who knows precisely what he is doing—writing an amusing trifle—and thoroughly enjoying the process.

V   The Humourous Courtier

The Humourous Courtier deals with the purging of a sick court. The title character, Orseola, is a declared misogynist at the court of the Duchess of Mantua. The Duchess has rejected the suit of the Duke of Parma, Foscari, who remains at her court disguised as Giotto. The Duchess is in love with someone at court, but she does not say who. The young lord Contarini thinks it may be himself, and he asks his wife of a month, Carintha, to commit suicide. The "young foolish lord" Depazzi courts Laura (" a young gentlewoman, great in favour") with claims to expertise in writing prayers, odes, satires, heroic poems, elegies, epigrams, and epitaphs.

The action moves in much the same manner as that of Ben Jonson's *Volpone*, with Depazzi, Contarini, and another young lord, Volterre, the dupes of a lighthearted, unwaspish Mosca, Foscari-Giotto. Orseola, too, allows himself to be deceived by Laura into thinking that the Duchess is mad for him. He counters a suggestion of impotency by revealing that he keeps a whorehouse of his own and pretends to hate women for fear of the Duchess's disfavor if she should learn of his satyriasis. Contarini arranges an assignation for Carintha and Giotto so that he can divorce her for adultery. Since the Duchess is going to announce her choice in the evening, there is not time for Contarini to divorce Carintha, so he asks her again to kill herself, and she agrees. He also asks Giotto to kill her, and Giotto agrees. The Duchess, however, chooses Giotto-Foscari, frustrating Contarini's plans. Foscari would not marry the Duchess until she purged her court of "humourous" characters.

The Humourous Courtier belongs in the tradition of Jonsonian comedy of humours. One of Shirley's less inspired efforts, it uses Jonson's technique without his insight into character. The satire of self-delusion makes little dramatic use of the way an unchecked natural inclination ("natural" to the individual temperament according to the degree to which a particular "humour" governs behavior) creates conflict. Shirley simply has his courtly characters unknowingly reveal their humours to the Duchess in the course of trying to win her favor. Desultory correction through exposure of their pretensions at the end of the play arbitrarily forces conformity to an unassailable code of desirable social behavior.

The impatience with individual differences evident here gives the impression that Shirley himself inclines toward authoritarianism. He does not attempt to suggest possible social reasons for the development of individual eccentricities. Humour is a "given," a physiological trait, added evidence that heredity, not environment, determines character. Individual human differences destabilize the kind of homogeneous society Shirley admires, and humours are to be dealt with summarily. The thesis of *The Humourous Courtier* may be legitimate, but Shirley does not explore it creatively; he is content to illustrate it with outré characters and situations.

VI The Traitor

The traitor of the title is Lorenzo, whose intrigues at the court of the Duke of Florence create strains on noble alliances between friends, between lovers, and between ruler and subject. Whether or not loyalty will crack under the strain determines the course of Shirley's tragedy here. Lorenzo's machinations test the moral strength of individuals in a community whose "ayre" is "infected" (II.i) as much by a selfish use of royal power (the Duke's) as by unscrupulous ambition (Lorenzo's).

The Duke owes his position to the overthrow of an earlier regime. He maintained his position against an "ambitious brother" and other threats to the peace with the help of his close friend ("I have worne him in my blood" [I.ii]), who is now plotting against him. Yet his position takes precedence over his character. The threat to peace preoccupies Shirley. The Duke may have serious shortcomings, and the virtuous Sciarrha who opposes him may be hot-bloodedly honorable, but while sympathy may be evoked for those who suffer injustice, as Sciarrha does, the safety of the structure of the commonwealth comes first. Order, however imperfectly sustained, is preferable to anarchy.

The case for anarchy is argued on a personal level by another virtuous courtier, Cosmo, who offers a rationale for inconstancy; he is joking, as it turns out.[10] Sciarrha, in a masque designed to warn the Duke against unruly behavior in a sovereign, has "Lust" urge: "Inflame but Kings with loose desire, / Yee soone set all the world on fire" (III.ii). Not Sciarrha, but Cosmo eventually restores order to a state disrupted as much by its leader's anarchic emotions as by Lorenzo's treason or Sciarrha's rebellion.

The disruption is violent. At the end of the play there are four corpses on stage, variously victims of a brother's sense of honor (Sciarrha kills his sister when she seems to be offering to sacrifice her virginity to save him), of assassination (Lorenzo murders the Duke), and of revenge (Sciarrha and Lorenzo kill each other). The last act has Lorenzo stabbing a picture of the Duke in anticipation of the actual murder and the Duke embracing the corpse of Sciarrha's sister before he discovers that she is dead. What leads up to the carnage can be traced partly to the rat race of court life (one courtier who wins the preferments he sought delivers a standard Renaissance plea for pastoral retirement, where one can be free of corruption and intrigue). But Shirley appears to be equally concerned with the violence of human emotion however or wherever stimulated. Codes of personal conduct designed to govern often ungovernable emotions figure as prominently in the action of the play as hierarchical laws guarding the head of state and his people. Shirley's tragic vision in *The Traitor* does not extend much beyond distrust of human emotion.

But his art allows for effectively theatrical individual scenes: a rejected young lady defers to her faithless lover's bride in elegantly funereal terms. She goes to "marry" Death, "whose lips though cold, / Distill chast kisses" (IV.ii). Depazzi, Lorenzo's creature, engages his servant in a witty charade before quitting court life forever. "What doe great Ladies doe at Court I pray?" asks Sciarrha rhetorically, launching a set speech (II.i) satirizing court decadence. And throughout the play Lorenzo defends himself against charges of treason or manipulates friends and enemies in utterances that cumulatively produce a "character" of the inveterate intriguer. *The Traitor* may not be good tragedy, but it offers much that is interesting, including several passages of quite felicitous verse.

CHAPTER 5

"Dancing Days": Plays 1633-1636

BETWEEN 1632 and 1636 Shirley wrote two masques, one short one (*A Contention for Honour and Riches*, not staged in the 1630s), and one a full-length successor to Jonsonian spectacle, *The Triumph of Peace*; this second masque was given a sumptuous production at Whitehall for the Inns of Court by Inigo Jones (see Chapter 2). Before plague closed the theaters again in 1636, Shirley also wrote at least eight plays for the Queen's men, *The Bird in a Cage*, *The Young Admiral*, *The Gamester*, *The Example*, *The Opportunity*, *The Lady of Pleasure*, *The Coronation*, and *The Duke's Mistress*. Standard classification of these plays by genre would designate *The Bird in a Cage*, *The Young Admiral*, *The Coronation*, and *The Duke's Mistress* as tragicomedies, and the others as city comedies. But *The Gamester* and *The Example* both have features usually associated with tragicomedy: the duel scene in *The Example* suggests that the play could take the direction of tragedy, and in *The Gamester* death is averted in the tragicomic manner. The liberties taken with city-comedy conventions in these two plays may mean dissatisfaction with or indifference to generic limitations; the amount and variety of Shirley's work from 1632 to 1636 clearly point to industry and versatility. The best of the work is *The Lady of Pleasure* (see Chapter 8), with *The Example* and *The Gamester* lesser achievements, but still superior to the rest of the group.

I The Example

The title, the action of the play, the names of the characters, and the epilogue all frankly announce a didactic purpose:

Wee must appeale to you, unles you smile
Wee have but cherish'd vain hopes all this while,
But if you like, by this we shall best prove it,
You'le follow THE EXAMPLE, if you love it. (Epilogue, last lines)

The Example teaches its lesson about faith and honor in a triple plot. In the main action Sir Solitary Plot's niece, Bellamia "of chaste honour" (Lady Peregrine, whose husband has lost his fortune and joined the army), accepts the gift of a jewel from Lord Fitzavarice, who holds a mortgage on Peregrine's lands.[1] Lady Plot gives Fitzavarice a key to Lady Peregrine's room. Bellamia's constancy transforms Fitzavarice, who had attempted a seduction: he gives her back the mortgage. Sir Walter Peregrine returns from the wars in the Lowlands and is about to leave again, when Lady Peregrine shows him the mortgage and tells him about the jewelry. He becomes angry when she reveals their benefactor's name. Sir Walter challenges Fitzavarice, but the latter's second, instead of arranging a duel, has Sir Walter arrested for debt. Fitzavarice has him released, but for the sake of their reputations insists upon the duel. They wound each other, but survive the encounter.

In the first subplot Sir Solitary suspects Lady Plot of an assignation with a poetaster, Confident Rapture. In the second subplot Vainman and Pumicestone, both courting a professed manhater, Jacinta, agree that whichever wins her must pay the other a thousand pounds. The girl, another niece of Sir Solitary, enjoins Vainman and Pumicestone to silence for six months, when she will choose between them. She tricks them into talking, and they become confirmed misogynists. Then Jacinta confesses to Lady Peregrine that she loves Fitzavarice, who proposes marriage. The Plots have reconciled, Sir Solitary realizing that he's been a "suspicious fool," and they end the play with a song.

The Example focuses clearly on the public and private dislocations attendant on deviation from traditional morality. If the theme of the play is "Whom can we trust?" then the example to follow is someone who trusts tradition. One of the characters in the play who does not is Confident Rapture, who speaks thus of Fitzavarice (before the unsuccessful attempt to seduce Lady Peregrine): "Bove all, he is adorer of chast truth, / And speakes religiouslie of any man. / Hee will not trust obscure traditions, / Or faith implicite but concluds of things / Within his owne clear knowledg" (II.i). After his rehabilitation Fitzavarice urges Lady Peregrine to "live, oh live," as the "best of wives," the example of whose faith "Hath purg'd the world, and taught us how to count / Our howers by thy miracles" (III.i). By the end of the play Fitzavarice, though still impressed by Confident Rapture's verse-making ability, adjures the poet to honesty, if he wants to continue to enjoy his patronage. Fitzavarice has set an example by his own reform. Confident Rapture, meaning to follow that example, perhaps represents the kind of writer in a time when the "new Philosophy calls all in doubt" who substitutes anarchic individualism for "obscure traditions" and "faith implicite" and is now ready to use his talent for what he once scorned.[2]

Confident Rapture's last-act promise to reform, prompted by the threat of losing patronage, may refer simply to cowardice and under-handedness. However, the character's machinations, essential to the development of the plot of *The Example*, have nothing to do with his being a poetaster. Shirley's choice of poetaster as intriguer may be arbitrary, or it may mean that through Confident Rapture he is exposing the degrading shifts to which even a debased talent must submit if it is to survive at all. It may even be that Shirley subconsciously is reflecting through Confident Rapture his own distress at the sometimes ignoble (never downright base or dishonest) uses to which he puts his talent. Confident Rapture's slavishly de-rivative and mindlessly distorted paeans to originality and individ-ualism (in morals and religion) before his promise to reform may reflect the unrecognized inner conflict of the strict traditionalist Shirley himself.[3]

II The Gamester

The Gamester develops the thesis that a reasonably madcap young Londoner can retain his spirit and his honor without breaking the law or risking his life.[4] Gaming itself is not necessarily antisocial. Good gamblers can be distinguished from bad. And a good gamester is also to be distinguished from a bravo, blade, or bully (such as a "Mohawk"); a good gamester is a gentleman. Barnacle, a wealthy citizen, is ambitious to make a gentleman, as he mistakenly under-stands one to be, out of his nephew. He pays Hazard, the gamester, to let the boy beat him in a public fight. Hazard carries out the charade with young Barnacle in a tavern. The boy learns quickly, too quickly, how to behave like a "gentleman"—so well, in fact, that his uncle pays Hazard to "unblade" the roaring hellion.

The gamester also figures in the main plot, which features misunderstandings among four couples, one of them married. Hazard manages to reconcile them all. For even if he is a "frolicsome fellow," "it followes not we should / Be mad out-right" (I.i). Spirited good humor should prevail over inclinations toward dueling or fighting of any kind among true gentlemen—who should also watch their language. Too often "gentlemen," complains Hazard, "cannot quarrell / About a glass of Wine, but out flies str[aight] / Sonne of a whore, dead mothers must be torne / Out of their graves, or living, have their names / Poysoned by a prodigious breath:" and he relates profane speech to unnecessary violence: "it were / A brave and noble Law to make this tongue / Be cut for't, it wod save much blood ith yeere, / That might be spent more honourablie" (I.i). Hazard himself is given to gaming with improvident lords, knights, and country gentlemen, merchants, wealthy young men-about-town, but he nevers utters a provocative word. He risks only money, not his integrity, and those who win from him or lose to him can learn to do so gracefully.

While offering a lesson in good manners, *The Gamester* also exploits Shirley's talent for racy dialogue. Hazard and a girl he describes as a "frosty gentlewoman" when he first sees her engage in amusingly risqué give-and-take:

Hazard.	This wench will jeere me.
Penelope.	I hope you are not one, sir.
Hazard.	One of what?
Penelope.	One of those honest men you talk'd of so,
	One to whose trust, a Virgin might commit
	A maiden-head, as you call it.
Hazard.	Yes, you may trust me.
	I have possest a hundred maiden-heads.
Penelope.	How long?
Hazard.	Nay, nay; they are no commodities to keepe,
	Noe fault of ours: truth is, th'are not worth
	Preserving, some of your owne Sex acknowledge it,
	And yet by your complexion, you have yours still;
	Away with 't, and in time.
Penelope.	Why you are modest. (III.i)

The lively language of this city comedy, relatively free from abstractions and clichés, has color and vitality, not unrelated to the author's sense of place. The long opening scenes of the first, fourth, and last acts take place in the street; four settings are interiors of private homes; two scenes are set in a tavern, and one in a prison. Long sentences in even the moralizing passages avoid subordination and read more like series of short simple sentences. The blank verse itself frequently has a colloquial lilt:

Wilding.   But harke thee, harke thee *Will*, did'st winne it [a wager]?
Hazard.   No, but I may loose it ere I goe to bed.
                Dost think it shall mustie, what's a hundred pound?
Sellaway.   A miracle, but they are ceast with me.
Hazard.   And me too, come lett's drinke. (II.ii)

The firm texture of Shirley's language in *The Gamester* allows for occasional loosening in the passages involving Leonora (who faints when she hears that her beloved Delamore has been "killed" in a duel), Violante (who grieves for Beaumont, arrested for "killing" Delamore), Mistress Wilding (who questions her husband's fidelity), and even the quick-witted virgin Penelope, when she and Hazard admit they love each other. The end product entertainingly fulfills serious intent by rendering a didactic tale in versatile dialogue that moves easily between the conversational and the declamatory. *The Gamester* may be burdened with too much moralizing, but much of the play is hearty city comedy. The comic cast of the whole colors even the relative drabness of the didactic passages.[5]

III   The Bird in a Cage

The loose form and varied texture of such plays as *The Bird in a Cage* suggest a lapse on Shirley's part, but *Bird* is actually more a vaudeville than a play, as much a theatrical piece in the tradition of hodgepodge entertainments (best exemplified in the English drama of a century earlier by Thomas Preston's *Cambyses*) as it is a contemporary phenomenon, a product designed to satisfy the taste for such curious artifacts as the masque, the Caroline predecessor of latter-day multimedia spectacles. *The Bird in a Cage* has no discernible structural principle governing the development of its action.

A young Mantuan, Philenzo, disguised as Rolliardo, wagers his life with his sweetheart's father, the Duke of Mantua, on his ability to enter the "New Prison," a castle in which the Princess Eugenia is to be sequestered until a proper marriage can be arranged. The sensibilities of Eugenia and Philenzo (heroic, virtuous, and ingenious enough to make true love laugh at locksmiths) occupy the dramatist in only two scenes, where the verse sounds lyrical without becoming strained or fatuous, something of an achievement considering the utter absurdity of the plot and the consequent effect upon the characterization of the lovers. When Eugenia sees the cage of birds the Duke has sent her as a present (he doesn't know Philenzo-Rolliardo is hidden inside), she addresses them plaintively: "Sweet fellow Prisoners, 'twas a cruel art, / The first Invention restraine the wing, / To keep th'inhabitants oth'ayre close Captive / That were created to Skye freedome." The sentiment, based on a simple enough identification ("fellow prisoners") and developed by the traditional contrast between "art" and nature, moves toward sentimentality: "surely / The mercilesse creditor took his first Light / And Prisons their first Models from such Bird Loopes; / I know yon Nightingale is not long-liv'd, / See how that Turtle mournes, wanting her Mate" (IV.ii). In a dramatic context as overburdened as *The Bird in a Cage* with artifice Eugenia appears to be attitudinizing; in themselves, the eight lines movingly mourn "the tears of things" deprived of freedom.

Between the first-act "imprisonment" of Eugenia and her last-act release, comic scenes, dances, and a play-within-a-play (about Jupiter and Danaë, the latter imprisoned by her father, King Acrisius) have more or less, usually less, to do with the development of the main plot. The spectacle of a cage of birds is prominent in the fourth act, where the hero does become involved. The climax has Philenzo concealed in the central pillar of the bird cage delivered to Eugenia. Whatever individual scenes (except those with the hero and heroine) have been concerned with, the fifth act concentrates on simply bringing the play to an end. The conduct of the action in *The Bird in a Cage* thus suggests that ordinary critical standards for judging plays might not apply.

The plot of *The Bird in a Cage*, no more absurd than many another devised by Shirley and others in his time and before it, should not be taken any more seriously today than it presumably was in the 1630s. Undoubtedly one could make a case for thematic relevance to contemporary social issues (tyranny of arranged marriages, perhaps), but the offhand, even tongue-in-cheek manner of the playwright here precludes a solemn critical approach. Consider the first-act concluding couplet, spoken by the would-be "spark" Morello (of whom another Mantuan courtier in the play has said, "the Court cannot subsist without a foole" [I.i]): "Like errand Knights, our valiant wits must wrastle / To free our Ladyes from the inchanted Castle."

The texture of *The Bird in a Cage* varies arbitrarily from Fletcherian romantic in the main plot to Jonsonian manic in the subplots. Like the scoundrels in Jonson's *The Alchemist,* Bonamico, an impoverished artist disguised as the mountebank Altomaro, hopes to repair his fortunes by selling his secret of invisibility to wealthy fools. Morello, one of these, dresses in women's clothes in an attempt to get past Eugenia's guards and join one of the ladies-in-waiting. One could argue that the invisibility and disguise elements in *The Bird in a cage* constitute variations on the Philenzo action, but it would be just as reasonable to see the play as undercutting its cruel dedication to the Puritan William Prynne, for his attacks on what he considered the decadence of royally approved productions like *The Bird in a Cage*.[6]

All the suspense and terror of tragedy in *The Bird in a Cage* are diluted by last-minute reprieves that belong to the world of tragicomedy, where an honorable but unfulfilled lover, an honorable but unappreciated courtier, scorns undeserved favor and risks death to win the loved one from whom he has been separated. Neither he nor she will do anything dishonorable, however nimbly they use their wits to prove stone walls do not a prison make that can keep them apart. They do struggle to win approval from the authority (parent and/or prince) responsible for their separation. In Shirley's tragedies they fail; in his tragicomedies, such as *The Bird in a Cage*, they succeed. The choice of genre, not any quality of character (the protagonists of the tragedies are often indistinguishable from those of the tragicomedies), would seem to determine the resolution of Shirley's actions.

IV The Young Admiral

The setting of this tragicomedy is ["Naples, and the Sicilian Camp"]. A great deal of exposition and incident is packed into the first scene, at the court of Naples. Vittori, the young admiral, can probably save Naples from invaders, but the prince Cesario is jealous of him: both are in love with Cassandra. Cesario has rejected the suit of the King of Sicily for his daughter Rosinda. The war between Naples and Sicily is a consequence of Cesario's punishment of a drunken Sicilian's rude remarks about Neapolitan women. Cesario appears to have had some difficulty returning home safely. He fears that another victory for Vittori will confirm his claim to Cassandra. Cesario is ready to sacrifice his country just to have her. Vittori's father, Alphonso, brings news of the young admiral's victorious return. Cesario deliberately baits him and has him arrested as a traitorous rebel.

The rest of the play, following this crowded first scene, develops an intricate plot very like that of an heroic play of the 1660s and early 1670s. Vittori and Cassandra struggle valiantly in choosing between love and honor. Their central scene (III.i) ends with Vittori saying, "to save / Her life, I bring my honour to the grave." The decision would be fatal for a tragic protagonist. In this tragicomedy, resourcefulness (including disguise) skirts the issue, solves the problem, ends the struggle. A comic subplot uses the same device, disguise: a lady-in-waiting got up as a witch gulls a foolish servant into believing he can become a military hero because he is immune to injury: "If the foole after this conceiving himselfe bewitch'd, should grow valiant, and doe wonders, who can helpe it?" (IV.i). Perhaps what Shirley had in mind was a demonstration of the wonders the truly valiant, unaided by magic, can accomplish.

The play has the usual Shirley quota of impassioned lyrical set pieces. Having chosen death before dishonor, Vittori means to comfort Cassandra when he declaims, "When I am dead the world shall doat on thee, / And pay thy beauty tribute"; the speech continues with an extravagant conceit: "A Sunne more glorious shall draw up thy teares / Which gracing heaven in some new forme, shall make / The Constellations blush, and envy em." The grand style persists in an imaginative flight that offers an alternative to forgetting: "let this comfort thee, / I die in my Countries Martyr and ascend / Rich in my scarlet robe of bloud"; yet with his next breath the self-proclaimed imminent martyr appears to be quite humble ("my name / Shall staine no Chronicle"). He will be content if his "Tombe be blest / With such a garland time shall never wither." The lengthy injunction ends with a hero's paradox: "Bid thee rejoyce, *Vittori* is a conqueror, / And death his way to triumph" (III.i). Scenes with speeches like this alternate with scenes of pure farce. Their juxtaposition alone does not imply an ironic approach or even a qualified endorsement of the heroic premise. The odd mixture did not displease Shirley's audience (Sir Henry Herbert, Master of the Revels, expresses admiration of the play in his notebook). And at least one modern commentator has commented on the superiority of *The Young Admiral* to its source, a play by Lope de Vega.[7]

As a tragicomedy, *The Young Admiral* sets up difficult choices for its protagonist, Vittori, but he never has to suffer their consequences. He suffers like any tragic hero, but only briefly. There is no question of his heroism, for he is ready to die honorably; the only doubts he allows himself have to do with what he should risk his life for. He does not analyze his motives; existence poses no riddles for him; his long speeches are designed to reveal his superior sensibilities. He can be passionate in his sense of injustice and even inveigh against his fate, but he never questions the moral basis of the social structure which produces that injustice. To justify his own decisions Vittori can present quite rational arguments, but these are largely rhetorical. He searches for ways out of his dilemmas, and his resourcefulness and a change in fortune ultimately provide solutions to apparently insoluble problems. Like all of Shirley's tragicomic protagonists, Vittori speaks sadly of his fate (or fortune), which remains inscrutable, but he does not question the nature, as he understands it, of whatever force is responsible for that fate or fortune.

V The Opportunity

This romantic comedy contains more disguises, mistaken identities, and impersonations than any other of Shirley's plays. Lucio, Pietro, and Julio, courtiers in Urbino, mistake Aurelio Andreozzi (visiting from Milan, traveling with his friend Pisauro and his servant Pimpinio; they are presumably on their way to war) for the banished Borgia (who never appears in the play). Aurelio goes to court with his "father," Mercutio, where Ursini, favorite of the reigning Duchess of Urbino, has no objection to "Borgia's" return. Ursini is in love with the real Borgia's sister, Cornelia. The Duchess gives Mercutio a pardon for Borgia; both she and Cornelia find Borgia-Aurelio attractive. Aurelio loves Cornelia and delays his consent to Ursini's suit for his "sister's" hand.

The Duke of Ferrara, disguised as his own ambassador, comes to court the Duchess for the Duke. He is displeased by her attentions to her new secretary, Aurelio. (Later in the play Pisauro will have Pimpinio impersonate Ferrara, to create "mirth.") The Duchess and Cornelia impersonate each other in conversations with Aurelio that Ferrara overhears. An innkeeper's mischievous son, disguised as a

"Switzer," urges Pimpinio, who considers himself a "natural prince," to seize an opportunity to win the Duchess's love: " 'Twere sinne to say shee'l honour you, for you / Are above all addition but her love; / Your wit, your blood, your person, doe not lose / The opportunitie" (III.i). The confusion of identity inevitably leads to emotional confusion. Order is restored when the truly "natural" nobility gravitate toward their own kind. Cornelia chooses Ursini even before the impersonations are exposed, and the Duchess chooses Ferrarra. Aurelio is pardoned for his impertinence, and the real Borgia is to return from exile in Naples.

The identity motif of *The Opportunity* could hardly help being germane to the meaning of a play whose theme is "Know your place and keep it." Aurelio takes advantage of an opportunity to improve his social position, although he is not entitled by birth to a high station in life. Most of the other characters, too, seize an opportunity when it presents itself to assume false identities, but for different reasons, sometimes just for the fun of it. Pimpinio, dressed "like a Spanish Don" and attended by "servants," clearly enjoys his opportunity to play a prince playing a fool for his "attendants." "Know thyself" for Shirley means knowing your place in a fixed social hierarchy. Mistaken identity can be an intrinsically funny theatrical device; in *The Opportunity* Shirley uses it exhaustively partly for purely comic purposes, but partly, too, to insist yet again that individual identity is best determined by birth and status. Individual fulfillment arises not from seizing opportunities to advance oneself beyond one's station, but from working faithfully and steadily within the limitations of one's social class.

The doctrine of privilege prevails, yet more than a hint of its vulnerability informs the characterization of the comic figure Pimpinio. In his impersonation of a member of a privileged class playing the fool at an inn, Pimpinio expresses a worm's-eye view of grandeur disassociated from honor. He practices the aristocratic manner, lofty condescension ("I am pleasd to reveal the majestie of my person" [III.i]), but not the principle of *noblesse oblige*. Pimpinio revels in a prince's right to whimsicality and capriciousness ("the toy may take me i'th head to looke like a foole agen"), but, unlike Shirley's genuinely honorable princely figures, the sense of duty eludes him. Thus, although "a Prince may play the foole" under certain conditions and a fool play a prince playing the fool, impersonation by a prince as well as by a fool necessarily means misrepresentation. The danger to the institution of royalty arises as much from a prince's catering to an uninformed concept of majesty as from a pandering like Pimpinio's to the prejudices of the crowd.

The guarded manner in which Shirley here presents his caveat to royalty may not have successfully concealed an offence inferred by the court. What has been called "a decline of his fortunes at court which began in 1634 and was the result of . . . his own frequent indulgence in satire of court life"[8] may be related to Shirley's practice in such a play as *The Opportunity* (1634). Since his firm commitment to the Royalist cause never wavered, the court's unfavorable reaction (if such were the case) to his discreet criticism of some of its more egregious follies seems out of proportion to the alleged *lèse majesté*. Or perhaps Shirley's vogue was simply being supplanted by another, as suggested by "the rapid rise to royal favor of William Davenant" at this time.[9]

VI The Coronation

For a solemn, near-tragic account of legitimate and spurious claims to earthly power, the tragicomedy *The Coronation* eschews comedy entirely. The prologue declares that "there doth flow / No undermirth, such as doth lard the scene / For course delight," but a comic treatment of the posturing figures in *The Coronation* might have enlivened this turgid exercise in court intrigue.[10]

Cassander, lord protector of Epire, looks forward to his son Lisimachus's marriage to the heir to the throne, Sophia. Her brothers, Leonatus and Demetrius, "nephews" of court nobles Eubulus and Macarius, respectively, are known as Seleucus and Arcadius, supposedly as unfriendly to each other as their fathers and "uncles." Sophia will not allow Arcadius to visit other courts. She wants to marry Lisimachus, but says the date depends on Cassander. He plans to crown her the next day and have her marry Lisimachus. She agrees to a duel between Seleucus and Arcadius even though, as she says, he "Hath no acquaintance yet with rugged warre, / More fit to drill a Lady than expose / His body to such dangers" (I.i), in order to settle the family feud. Macarius and Eubulus plead with Sophia to cancel the duel, but, when she does not, they plan to circumvent her decision.

After Sophia has been crowned, Cassander is to continue in a position of great power, but she makes it clear to all that she means to rule. Surprisingly, she chooses Arcadius, not Lisimachus, as her consort. A bishop reveals that Arcadius is Sophia's youngest brother,

Demetrius. She gives him the crown. But there is to be a third coronation. The new king, Arcadius, declines Cassander's offer to continue in the protectorate and has him sent to a house that he plans to attack, Cassander having falsely led him to believe that a revolution was brewing there. The bishop reveals, and Eubulus admits, that Seleucus is Leonatus, whose dying father had concealed his and Demetrius's identities for fear of Cassander's ambition. Leonatus, the natural superior of his passive brother, is also the rightful king.

The Coronation develops a thesis almost obsessive with Shirley: blood will tell. The premise of divine right is reinforced. What was treated comically in *The Opportunity* (unwillingness to accept the position in life that one is born to) becomes matter for near-tragedy in *The Coronation*, for while temporary social dislocations can be amusing, failure to acknowledge natural leadership in the supreme representative on earth of the Supreme Being violates the sanctity of heavenly mandate.

As a dramatic paradigm of consecrated royalty, *The Coronation* has courtiers reminding the heir to the throne "Your power on earth's divine" and "Princes are here / The Coppies of eternity." The royal presence makes itself felt with such expressions as "We are not pleasd" and "We would be private" (I.i). Among themselves the Queen's subjects urgently inquire into her health, her moods, her appearance ("how lookes the Queene / This golden morning?" [II.i]). Encounters with her pander to "royal privilege," which will brook no "unreverend boldness" from even the most loyal. Too great emphasis on the deference due royalty produces a fatuous tribute to the institution and makes of *The Coronation* a humorless caricature of court life.

Moreover, the central conflict of the play is dealt with speciously. "Seleucus"-Leonatus soliloquizes:

> Why was I borne to be a subject? 'tis
> Soon answer'd, sure my Father was no Prince,
> Thats all, the same ingredience use[d] to make
> A man, as active, though not royall blood
> Went to my composition. (IV.i)

He is affirming a principle of natural superiority as the logical basis for determining who shall lead, who shall follow. When he discovers who he really is, Leonatus declares:

> there were seeds
> Scatterd upon my heart, that made it swell
> With thought of Empire, Princes I see cannot
> Be totally eclipst.

And in his next speech he recognizes that "Nature has rectifi'd in me . . . The wandrings of ambition" (V.iii). To create a genuine conflict, a real commoner would be pitted against a prince of equally outstanding qualities. But "Seleucus" is really Leonatus, the legitimate heir to the throne of Epire. Thus the play works to demonstrate the natural superiority of princes whose identity may be concealed, but whose nature marks them as nobly born.

VII   The Duke's Mistress

To judge by the prologue, Shirley had little hope of success for *The Duke's Mistress*, the last of his plays to be produced in London before he left for Ireland, since in it he was not accommodating the taste, as he perceived it, of the majority of London theatergoers ("the generall guests to Playes") in the mid-1630s for "Satire, and wantonnes," "two straines: that please." The opening scene raises moral issues (marital fidelity and constancy contrasted with fair-weather friendship) immediately. Courtiers Valerio and Silvio mean to follow their Duke's example in avoiding Dionisio Farnese's abused Duchess Euphemia now that she is out of favor. Dionisio's favorite, Leontio, jeopardizes his position at court by his friendliness to her. From the outset, then, the play addresses itself to a court situation of apparently limited interest to audiences of the time.

The rest of the main action of this tragicomedy develops its theme in a series of highly melodramatic gestures that never result in catastrophe for anyone but the villain of the piece, Valerio. Euphemia first begs Dionisio to kill her, then swears revenge. The Duke places her in Leontio's custody. Dionisio has been advancing a "noble gentleman," Bentivolio, in the hope that he might persuade Ardelia to submit to the Duke. Valerio, a scoundrel at court, who exploits the most intimate secrets, reveals Bentivolio's real love for Ardelia to the Duke, tries to blackmail Ardelia into an affair, and then enters into a conspiracy with Bentivolio and Leontio to kill the Duke. Ardelia threatens Valerio with a gun. He "Goes behinde the hangings" as Bentivolio enters. Bentivolio kills Valerio, thinking he is killing the Duke. When the would-be assassin whom Leontio hired tells him that he has killed the Duke and has a troubled conscience, Leontio sends Ardelia and Bentivolio off to prison. But the Duke is not dead, he and Euphemia are reconciled, and all ends happily for everyone but the villainous Valerio.

The subplot bears little thematic relationship to the main plot and might even be considered in bad taste. According to Horatio, friend of Bentivolio, one cannot expect a beautiful woman to be true. Horatio says he prefers ugly women, like Fiametta, to the lovely court ladies Aurelia and Macrina, and tries to get Bentivolio to forget Ardelia. Horatio will prove to be mistaken in his distrust of beauty, for the beautiful Ardelia is not the Duke's mistress, and he will voluntarily join Ardelia and Bentivolio in prison to escape Fiametta. The correlation of great physical beauty with high moral character means that the ugly Fiametta is abandoned when Horatio ultimately admits that a woman can be beautiful and chaste: cynical men are to blame when beautiful women go astray.

Equally disconcerting as Horatio's proposition and its reverse is the double standard of morality for the virtuous characters and for the villain, Valerio. Valerio means to make use of Bentivolio's confession of love for Ardelia, for only true friends and lovers can open their hearts freely to each other with no fear of betrayal. Yet Bentivolio needs the evidence he gains from eavesdropping to believe that Ardelia is not the Duke's mistress. The abused Duchess Euphemia alone will not exploit an intimate revelation. Leontio's declaration of love for her elicits a rather violent affirmation of her marriage vows. Leontio, on the other hand, may try to free her from them by having Dionisio killed.

Leontio may scheme and plot and intrigue and escape retribution, but not Valerio. The "mistery of fate" that Valerio speaks of as he dies appears to be quite arbitrary, but he perceives it as God's justice: "I am caught in my owne toyles, by the same Engine / I rais'd to the *Dukes* death, I fall my selfe." He "wo'd looke up, and beg with my best strength / Of voyce, and heart forgivenes, but heaven's just, / Thus death payes treason, and blood quencheth lust" (V.i). Because *The Duke's Mistress* is a tragicomedy, in it a just God punishes villains. The innocent may suffer temporarily, as Ardelia does, but their suffering only tests their faith. A merciful God will protect them and reward them for their fortitude and endurance. Similarly he will forgive breaches of faith in the virtuous, such as Leontio.

Valerio's last speech properly belongs to a more complex character than Shirley conceived. The equally amoral Iago of *Othello* goes to his death unrepentant, with no more sense of divine retribution at the end of his infamous career than at the beginning. Marlowe's Faustus (of whose last speech Valerio's is reminiscent) has always been aware of the consequences of his unholy alliance. Shirley provides no hint of the source of Valerio's sudden insight into the workings of Providence; the tragicomic convention itself may be held responsible for the simplistic resolution of the complicated plot, but not for the villain's subscribing to the idea of poetic justice. Shirley must be held responsible for faulty characterization here in a context cloudy with contradictions.

CHAPTER 6

"The Throes and Travail of a Teeming Brain": Plays 1637-1639

SHIRLEY'S "dancing days" in London came to an end with the outbreak of another epidemic in 1636. He left for Ireland at the behest of John Ogilby, tutor to the family of the Lord-Lieutenant of Ireland, Lord Strafford. Ogilby "erected the only pre-Restoration theater outside of Londin, in Dublin"[1] on Werburgh Street. Shirley lived in Dublin for four years. During his stay there Jonson died in London (1637), and the poet-laureateship of England, for which Shirley had been considered, was awarded (1638) to William Davenant.

The hard-working playwright was as active in Dublin as ever he had been in London. He produced eight new plays, *The Royal Master, The Gentleman of Venice, The Doubtful Heir, St. Patrick for Ireland, The Constant Maid, The Politician*, and two plays that were never printed, a tragedy, *St. Albans*, and a comedy, *Look to the Ladie;* and eight more plays (for which Shirley wrote prologues) by Jonson, Beaumont and Fletcher, Middleton, and other, less well known, contemporary English dramatists.[2] Shirley's industry is all the more striking in that his "productions were poorly attended."[3] In spite of "spectacular display of costume, entertainment, and stage effects,"[4] his productions attracted few Dubliners outside of the small English population, and Shirley "complained of inadequate public support and empty seats."[5] The plays Shirley wrote in Ireland include two designed to attract Irish audiences, *St. Patrick for Ireland* and *The Doubtful Heir*, which has an "Irish" subplot.[6]

Of the six extant plays from Shirley's Irish period, the romantic comedy *The Gentleman of Venice* and the city comedy *The Constant*

99

Maid rank among the best of Shirley's work in their respective genres. The other four plays belong among his competently executed endeavors in tragicomedy and tragedy.

I   The Gentleman of Venice

The changeling fable provides Shirley with yet another opportunity in *The Gentleman of Venice* to dramatize the thesis that blood will tell. Giovanni and Thomazo, exchanged in infancy by Ursula, wet-nurse and mother, respectively, reveal their true origins through choice of companions (Giovanni, growing up as a Duke's gardener's son, searches out learned men among the aristocracy and falls in love with the Duke's ward, Bellaura; Thomazo, as the Duke's son, follows the lead of Malipiero, spendthrift and whoremonger) and capacity for heroism (Giovanni goes to war and returns victorious; Thomazo shirks military duty). Shirley subscribes unequivocally to the notion that heredity, and not environment, determines character. Counterpoint to the development of his thesis is the pervasive imagery of gardens, cultivation, and growth.

Depending on who the gardener is, gardening is associated with drudgery or aristocratic taste. Giovanni's topiary designs include lions and unicorns, crowns, and coats of arms; for the servant Georgio gardening is "course-work" (I.ii). The garden is Giovanni's "Academy" (II.i), for there he listens to and observes fine ladies and gentlemen. The court is a "glorious Landschape" (II.i) to him. Malipiero provokes a fight by referring to Giovanni as belonging to a "dunghill breed": " 'Tis a base employment, / Fit for such a drudge as *Giovanni*. . . . Dee scorn youre [dunghill breed]?" (II.i) Ironically, Thomazo precipitated the insult by challenging the English gentleman Florelli to a flower-bed-digging contest. Thomazo comes by his taste "naturally," as it turns out. In the fight that follows Malipiero's insult, Giovanni first uses a spade, then a sword. Later, Bellaura reacts to his enlistment in the army with "your weapon is a spade I take it" (III.ii). "You love a growing vertue," Giovanni tells her guardian, Contarini, the Duke of Venice (Giovanni's real father), who responds, "This Giovanni? / His words tast more of courtier then the Garden" (IV.ii). Giovanni refuses monetary reward for his military service: "alas I rise / Like a thin reede beneath this Common-wealth" (IV.ii). When he balks at preferment for one "low born," the Duke says, "We look not at thy root, but at thy blossom"

(IV.ii). Rejected by Bellaura, Giovanni means to return "to the Garden . . . and there begin / Another grouth" (IV.ii).

Elsewhere the garden imagery figures incidentally in the development of minor and related themes. Cornari sends a noose to his despised nephew, Malipiero, for hanging himself: there is one tree in Cornari's orchard he "would have bear no other fruit" (III.i). Cornari rationalizes his scheme to have a stranger father a child on his wife, Claudiana, by insisting on her right to the kind of immortality having a child would bring: "So rich a blessing, rather like a plant / Should root, and grow, and bloom, & bear for ever" (IV.i). In the scene preceding Ursula's revelation of her deception, responding to her gardener-husband Roberto's refusal to take her to court to plead for Thomazo, she threatens to "spoile the Garden, / Break up the hedges, and deface the works / Your darling *Giovanni* made" (V.i). Highborn Bellaura early on discovers lowborn Georgio's knack for repartee and engages him in an amusing battle of wits about gardens:

Bellaura.	Why you are conceited [clever] sirra, does wit Grow in this Garden?
Georgio.	Yes, Madam while I am in't, I am a slip Myself.
Bellaura.	Of Rosemary or time [thyme]?
Georgio.	Of wit sweet Madam.
Bellaura.	'Tis pitty, but thou shouldst be kept with watering.
Georgio.	There's wit in every Flower, if you can gather it.
Bellaura.	I am of thy mind. But what's the wit prethee of yonder tulip?
Georgio.	You may read there the wit of a young Courtier.
Bellaura.	What's that?
Georgio.	Pride, and shew of colours, a fair promising, Deare when 'tis bought, and quickly comes to nothing.
Bellaura.	The wit of that rose?
Georgio.	If you attempt, Madam to pluck a rose [use a privy], I shall find a moral in't.
Bellaura.	No Country wit?

Equally well integrated as the garden imagery into the overall deterministic design of *The Gentleman of Venice* is the Cornari plot, which, like the subplot of Middleton and Rowley's *The Changeling*, most commentators well into the twentieth century have found deplorable. Arthur H. Nason does acknowledge that the Cornari and Giovanni plots are "skilfully interwoven": "Malipiero, especially,

constitutes a lively connecting link between the two actions: he is
the occasion of the Cornari-plot; and his escapade with the duke's
supposed son, Thomazo, brings about the revelation that solves the
Giovanni-plot."[7] But evidence of Shirley's dramaturgic skill does not
affect Nason's judgment of the Cornari action, which he finds "con-
spicuously repulsive" (p. 305). He repeats the indictment frequently, with almost every critical comment on *The Gentleman of
Venice* in his book: "repulsiveness of this . . . action" (p. 306);
"repulsive element" (p. 312); "the tainted atmosphere of *The Gentleman of Venice*" (p. 314); "in so far as it deals with the endeavors of
Cornari, it has a repulsiveness that neither the dramaturgic skill of
Shirley nor the virtue of Cornari's wife can soften" (p. 319); *The
Gentleman of Venice* is listed among three plays "repulsive in ma-
terial" (p. 319); the play combines "with excellence of treatment an
extreme repulsiveness of subject-matter" (p. 320); "the repulsiveness of *The Gentleman of Venice*" (p. 381).

The alleged repulsiveness of the Cornari action requires some
attention. Cornari (= to be cuckolded), unable to father a child
himself and unwilling to leave his fortune to his dissipated nephew
Malipiero, devises a scheme for inseminating his wife through a
handsome foreign visitor and then killing him. The scheme fails,
because the intended adulterers prove to be too virtuous. "Providence / Chain'd up our blood" (V.ii), Florelli tells Cornari (in disguise as a monk). He and Claudiana spent their time together
praying for Cornari's conversion. And when Malipiero (unaccount-
ably) reforms, there is no longer any reason for Cornari to divert
the inheritance or to deplore his childlessness. Certainly Shirley
characterizes Cornari as repulsive, but apparently neither the dramatist nor his audience was squeamish about the action involving
Cornari. And there is more to the relationship between the Cornari
and Giovanni plots than Malipiero. Both involve tests of the nature
of true parentage. Given Shirley's bias toward the superiority of
noble birth, it is no wonder that he should arrange a plot suggesting
at first that a gardener's son may through cultivation alone win
elevation to the nobility, but ultimately revealing Giovanni as the
Duke's real son. The failure of Cornari's scheme emphasizes the
futility of attempts to disguise the provenance of gentle birth.

Shirley asks not "What makes a gentleman?" but "What is a
gentleman?" Roberto indulges his "son" Giovanni's gentlemanly
pursuits over the objection of Ursula, who knows that the real gentleman is Giovanni, and not her substitute Thomazo. Giovanni's gen-

tlemanliness puzzles highborn and lowborn alike, for a gentleman should be immediately recognizable to his peers and inferiors. The Englishman Florelli has "in's face the promise / Of a most noble nature" (I.iii), according to the gentlemen of Venice, whom he commends for their courtesy and graciousness. Giovanni is a gentleman, not because he learned gentlemanliness "at those schooles / Of wit and action" (II.i), the Academies, but because he was born the son of a Duke. "The helpes of Education . . . seldome / Do correct nature," observes Contarini's "courtier of honour," Marino (V.iv).

A minimum of such sententiousness about matters dear to Shirley's heart appears in *The Gentleman of Venice,* matters such as the nature of true nobility and the proper social roles for members of strictly segregated classes. The unconfined ambience perhaps accounts for the spirited tone of the play. The action of the first six scenes, half the play, takes place outdoors, in the streets (including the Rialto) of Venice and in the gardens of the Duke. With Scene III.i the action moves indoors (except for V.i and V.iii) for the rest of the play, which ends in an apartment of the Duke's palace. Certainly the familiar character types and the theatrical plot inventions benefit from the open-air lustiness of Ursula, Georgio, and Malipiero, for Giovanni remains a highly idealized (and in this play dramatically successful) projection of Shirley's notion that ancestry (blood, breeding), not nurture, determines character.

II   The Constant Maid

The Constant Maid rivals and almost matches *The Opportunity* for the distinction of most contrived and cluttered comedy in Shirley's canon. The development of the plots and "cross-plots" in *The Constant Maid* features eavesdropping, feigned madness, disguise, espionage, gulling and duping, testing of lovers' faithfulness, misunderstandings, and last-act revelations. Possibly influenced by Richard Brome's comedies, the play is an epitome of Caroline comic structure.

The setting is London "and the fields adjoining." A young gentleman, Hartwell, in an economical move, dismisses his servants, but old Close, who had also served his father, asks to stay on. The rest join a "young Gallant," Playfair, in an obscure "rewarding project," a get-rich-quick enterprise. Hartwell loves Frances, daughter of a rich widow, Mistress Bellamy, who would approve of the match except that Hartwell is "poor." The widow maintains a lavish household only according to the usurer Hornet; practical concerns about money lead her to advise Frances not to marry the handsome but impecunious Hartwell: "they are not Kisses / Will arme you against winter" (I.ii). Later she tells Hartwell that she wants him for herself. The proposal "destroys" Hartwell. Frances fares no better, for her mother seems to be hoping for a match between Frances and a foolish, but wealthy, country gentleman, Startup.

Playfair advises Hartwell how to deal with Mistress Bellamy. He himself is in love with the usurer Hornet's niece. Startup tells Frances what he learned from her Nurse, who overheard Playfair and Hartwell talking about Hartwell's wanting to marry Frances's mother. The Nurse schemes with Startup and Close to get Startup into Frances's bed (Close is involved because his master, Hartwell, plans to take Startup's place). When the time comes, Close gulls Startup into thinking Hartwell is after him, and so clears the way for Hartwell to enter Frances's bedroom with the Nurse's help. The Nurse tells Frances that Mistress Bellamy has been testing Hartwell. Frances wonders if he has been pretending to love her mother. The Nurse brings in Hartwell disguised as Startup, but Frances recognizes him. Mistress Bellamy reveals to Frances that she was indeed testing Hartwell—and Frances's constancy. Playfair has married Hornet's niece, who joins him in a masque attended by Hornet. Hartwell, wearing Startup's clothes, is arrested on suspicion of murder. He is cleared, and all the play's other entanglements are unsnarled in the last scene. Even Hornet converts from usury to charity, or, as Playfair puts it, "Ye are the first / Jew that in my remembrance has turn'd Christian" (V.iii).

The plot is negligible; more interesting is the play's vivid image of London life. *The Constant Maid* abounds in topical allusions ranging from whimsical comments on London fashions of the 1630s ("hospitalitie / Went out of fashion with . . . cod-peeces" [I.i]) to sentimental reminders of popular plays: Ben Jonson's *The Case Is Altered* and *The Sad Shepherd;* Thomas Kyd's *The Spanish Tragedy* (still occasionally revived and apparently remembered warmly more than fifty years after its original production); Shakespeare's *Much Ado About Nothing* (Verges); and the much more recent *Perkin Warbeck* of John Ford. References to the theater outnumber those to any other institution of the time. The self-consciousness suggested here about the theatricality of the play's action makes the improbable plot almost incidental to the evocation of lively London life.

Rather more notorious London institutions than the theater receive some attention: Bedlam, Bridewell, and the entry to St. Paul's Cathedral, where rascals gathered. Apprentices (who rioted on Shrove Tuesdays) and pawnbrokers, though they do not figure in the plot, belong to the world of a play that involves master-servant relationships (Hartwell-Close) and get-rich-quick schemes (Playfair and Hartwell's discharged servants). And the legend of Dick Whittington and his cat, almost as old as Magna Charta *(sic)*, was still as much a part of contemporary consciousness as the Star Chamber (cited for its power, not the terrible reputation it has since earned).

The world outside London is mentioned only a few times: a passing glance at Spain and the Low Countries; a sprinkling of learned, but by no means esoteric, classical allusions (Jove and Juno, Venus, Cupid, Mercury, Pluto, Pythagoras); cliché treatment of Machiavel(li). A taste for the paintings of Michael Angelo *(sic)* was as much a mark of wealthy Londoners' cultivation as that for marchpane (marzipan), tobacco, and the coranto (a dance). Shirley's concern for London atmosphere in *The Constant Maid* allows for some interest in foreigners past and present, but remains essentially parochial.

In this affectionate tribute to London Shirley skillfully reshuffles a dog-eared pack of city-comedy situations and "special" features, including yet another masque of three goddesses contending for a golden apple. If the play lacks originality, it reads, and probably played, as well as any other of Shirley's works in this genre. In fact *The Constant Maid* reaches a little higher than the experienced craftsman's usual level of competence. The prolific Shirley, as relatively productive in the much smaller, narrower theater world of Dublin as in that of London, by the late 1630s had developed a facility that stood him in good stead when he wrote innocuous entertainments like *The Constant Maid*. Perhaps absence from his beloved London accounts for Shirley's reaching almost a lyrical level (unusual in city comedy) in his fond recollections of familiar London landmarks.

III   The Politician

Among the last of Shirley's plays to be produced in Dublin before he returned to England was *The Politician,* usually listed among his tragedies, probably because the title character precipitates the action that leads to his destruction. But similar characters in the tragicomedies may die (Valerio in *The Duke's Mistress*) or escape death

(Montalto in *The Royal Master*), and Gotharus is no more prominent in the action of *The Politician* than the villains in the tragicomedies. Whether the play is properly designated a tragedy or a tragicomedy matters less, however, than its classification as a moral-didactic dramatization of the danger unbridled political ambition and undisciplined court behavior pose to monarchy.

Near the beginning of the play a brief appearance by Gotharus, the King of Norway's counselor, frowning at nameless petitioners, establishes him quickly as an angry, dangerously powerful politician manipulating the lives and fortunes of great and small alike. The term "politician" (or "polititian," as it is spelled in the first edition, 1655) meant "a shrewd schemer; a crafty plotter or intriguer" in Shirley's time. Gotharus's presence certainly captures the spotlight while he is on stage, but it is only a small part of a long scene ultimately more concerned with the court as a whole than with Gotharus.

A cynical tone marks the crowded opening exposition of the troubled Norwegian court. In a gallery of the King's palace two courtiers, Cortes and Hormenus, discuss the tangled relationships of the monarch, his son, his favorite counselor (Gotharus), the latter's wife, the new Queen, her dead husband, her son—all in a little over two pages of dialogue. The prospect of a court in the process of destroying itself by its preoccupation with personal problems accounts for the cynicism. Later scenes penetrate beyond the court to the larger community necessarily affected by friction among the kingdom's leaders.

The first eruption of Gotharus's evil may destroy his loving, innocent wife. "I first / Practise at home," he admits in soliloquy (I.i), after dealing cruelly with Albina, fresh from an indecent proposal from the King of Norway. He is quite prepared to use her as he used the new Queen, Marpisa ("From whom I took my first ambition"), and as he intends to use all "till we can sway the Kingdom, / Though we climb to't o're many deaths." The action proper of the play confirms the truth of Cortes and Hormenus's exchange and dramatically justifies the cynical tone of the detailed exposition. A series of briskly written scenes, beginning with the second act (like the first a single scene), reveals the Norwegian court as an intricate network of intrigue.

For most of the play the maneuverings of court figures appear to be wholly confined to the interests of the high and the mighty, but with the supposed death of the heir to the King of Norway's throne

(IV.iv), the "common people" suddenly appear on the scene. Bent on revenge, they assault Gotharus's house. The unnamed rebels are under Duke Olaus's control, but their presence, like that of Olaus and his army, extends the meaning of the play's action beyond the confines (sometimes stultifying in Shirley's court plays) of the court.

Within the court the round of drunkenness, adultery, disguise, poisoning, shooting, and feigned death produces a violent atmosphere of treachery and deceit, associated, perhaps surprisingly, with elegant language. Olaus, the King's uncle and commander of the army, compares witty courtiers unfavorably to plain-speaking soldiers like himself: "Although we ha' not the device of tongue / And soft phrase Madam" (he is addressing Queen Marpisa), "which you make an Idol / At Court, and use it to disguise your heart, / We can speak truth in our unpollish'd words" (III.1).[8] Courtly manners are degenerating, however. They desert even the King, who cuffs two of his clownish lords, one of whom also takes a beating from a soldier of Olaus—who himself strikes one of his officers.

Although the playwright might very well have been simply dramatizing the danger to king and country of ambitious intriguers, *The Politician*, unless very carefully staged, could easily become farce in the theater, even in Shirley's time. We would be mistaken to attribute a black-comic intention to Shirley here, yet the knockabout action at least makes the stately passages suspect, especially when Olaus surrenders the coffin in which Gotharus is hiding to "the Rabble," "the devouring multitude," who think that their beloved prince Turgesius lies dead inside and mean to bury him in defiance of the King (Olaus has told them that the King forbade "rights of funerall"). The King himself is reduced to railery at the beginning of the last act and to self-pity when he thinks that Olaus has taken away his kingdom ("To whom now must I kneel? Where is the King? / For I am nothing, and deserve to be so" [V.ii]). He whines as he contemplates "the miserable fate of Kings." A king's death is a "sacrifice" to "murmuring" subjects. Written when the King of England was indeed in danger from his subjects, such a speech— and such a mixed bag of raucousness and stateliness as *The Politician*—seems to beg for derision as it ruefully perceives the tenuousness of kingly sway.

The Politician is not black comedy; it is not, however, a tragedy either, even though the title page of the 1655 edition of the play refers to it as such, and in spite of several deaths, including that of the title character. The mock deaths of Turgesius and Aquinas;

Turgesius's hope of marrying Gotharus's innocent widow, Albina; and the King's survival of the rebellion all serve the tragicomic tradition. The King suffers only briefly for poor judgment (trusting Gotharus; marrying Marpisa) and for straying from the path of virtue (pursuing Albina). Along the way an innocent, Haraldus, and the foolish Helga and Sueno die, but they are minor characters. The deaths of Gotharus and Marpisa, out-and-out villains, driven by insatiable ambition, remove major threats to the status quo. The plainspoken soldier Olaus has outwitted the fancy talkers and saved the kingdom. The tragicomic reversals prove to be the consequences of Olaus's carefully laid secret plans to undermine the master intriguer, the politician Gotharus, at his own game. Presumably there will no longer be any reason for Cortes and Hormenus to gossip cynically about court affairs. Loyal courtiers, such as Olaus, Turgesius, and Aquinas, plot and counterplot only against ambitious traitors, and these are dead, like the villainous Valerio at the end of the tragicomedy *The Duke's Mistress*.

The Politician, whose authorship has never been disputed,[9] has three scenes (the fourth, fifth, and sixth in the fourth act) uncharacteristic of Shirley's style in plays with settings at a royal court. These scenes are full of violent action of the kind to be found in such plays set in London as *The Gamester*. However desperate the measures taken by villains at court, Shirley usually mutes their violence on stage, even in the (allegedly) Websterean tragedy, *The Cardinal*. Still, most of *The Politician* reads very much like others of Shirley's plays and should continue to be attributed to him.

IV The Royal Master

Shirley's Irish period includes yet another glorification of royalty, *The Royal Master*. The King of Naples, conceived of as the image of God's power on earth, is largely characterized by his own speeches on kingship: "We may be just . . . / Yet not destroy another attribute, / Which shewes whose representative we are; / Mercy becomes a King" (V.i). "I must not, dare not pardon," he declares in this first scene of the last act; " 'twere a sinne / In me of violence to heaven and justice." And the faithless Montalto, his onetime favorite, now to be exiled, responds, "You have beene a Royall Master." The royal master has the last lines of the play, a tragicomedy that ends the way it does because the King has tempered justice with mercy (Montalto's life is spared, but he is exiled from

Naples). The play works to reconcile a variety of loves and ambitions to the welfare of a court where individual fortunes in love and power rise and fall according to the disposition of its prince.

The Duke of Florence and Theodosia, sister of the King of Naples, a widower and the Duke's brother-in-law, appear to be destined for marriage. Montalto, the King's favorite, opposes the alliance. Both the King and the Duke are in love with Domitilla, who says she loves the King. And, according to Montalto, Theodosia is in love with someone other than the Duke. Montalto implies that she is no virgin—that he has been her lover. Evil wears an attractive face, as deceptive as Montalto's quick mind: only the undeceived Duke of Florence addresses him as *"Deare Machiavill"* (IV.i).

A more worthy courtier, Octavio, is in love with Domitilla, who admits she loves him, though she is ambitious to be queen. The Duke and King reveal their misgivings. A letter from Theodosia about her love for the Duke does not affect his decision to break their engagement, for he now believes her not to be chaste. When the King tells Theodosia that the Duke loves Domitilla, Theodosia decides on revenge. Then she learns that Domitilla loves the King, and the two young women suffer together. The King tells Montalto to marry Domitilla. His favorite is reluctant, but wants only to serve his King, he says, so he agrees. Montalto is full of schemes, plots, and intrigues that will strengthen or protect his position at court if they are successful. The King's judgment, it would seem, failed him when he favored Montalto. Or perhaps Montalto was too clever for him. There is no questioning of authority here, no aspersion cast on kingship, no doubts about the desirability of a monarchy, indeed no real questions even about Naples's judgments. The evil of Montalto is responsible for the trouble at the King's court, as Satan's is in God's earthly court.

The King plays right into Montalto's hands. Thinking his sister is unchaste, he wants to marry her off to him. When Montalto agrees, the King is grateful, but can think of no apt reward. He suggests a way for Montalto to find out who are his true friends: he will appear to have lost the King's favor. The last act has Domitilla rejecting the Duke, who now finds Theodosia attractive. Having seen her at first only as a partner in an agreement to join Naples and Florence in a convenient political alliance, he had taken her for granted. He realizes that he might have found her as attractive as she found him if their alliance had not been prearranged. By this time Montalto no longer has to pretend that he has lost the King's favor: he does lose it; he is banished from the court; his followers, too, are exiled. The King has been testing Domitilla, has found her honorable, and now gives her to Octavio. The central character, the royalmaster, thus functions as deus ex machina. His only human fault was trusting an attractive rascal. Tragicomic convention, however, allows a plot contrivance that reveals Montalto's true nature in time for the King to avert catastrophe.

Until his fall from the royal master's graces, Montalto is presented not only as the cleverest of the courtiers, but also as the most articulate in expressing the court's highest ideals. In the course of the play he gives the most lyrical speeches on love and honor. The villain of *The Royal Master* delivers the finest set piece in the play, on the beauty and terror in the natural sequence of sunlight and cloud (II.ii). The assignment of this passage to Montalto suggests a more complex and subtle characterization than Shirley offers elsewhere in the play. If the poetic flight reflects the Montalto-Royal Master relationship, then the villain of the piece is ironically contemplating his own villainy, wryly projecting himself as a threat to Naples: he is the "cloud" bringing a "storm" that leaves the "flattering day" in "ruines," for the court (the "faire sky"), the King ("the glorious Sunne"), and the citizenry ("every creature" on "the bosome of the earth"). In the end it is the flatterer who is ruined, and the benign influence of the sun that prevails: only for Montalto has the day's beauty been deceptive. Montalto's speech, fine in itself, unfortunately points up by comparison *The Royal Master's* otherwise pedestrian treatment of seventeenth-century court intrigue.

V   St. Patrick for Ireland

That Shirley's practice of tailoring plays to suit popular taste gives evidence of professional hackwork would be the contention of scholars like Hugh MacMullan, whose commentary on *St. Patrick for Ireland* includes this statement: "The poet has taken the life of the Saint and by use of the contemporary drama, has translated that life into a typical tragi-comedy whose chief protagonist is a religious person. . . ."[10] A more lenient judgment of the play might find it as close to *The Second Shepherds' Play* and other fifteenth-century plays less artistically fashioned as to Stuart drama. A mixture of sacred and profane, with many loose ends, *St. Patrick,* it is true, uses the legend only as a prop on which to build a plot involving

true and false lovers and loyal and unfaithful courtiers. But most of
the play features what MacMullan probably rightly considers ac-
commodation of the taste in 1639 for "surprize in plot and a baroque
decoration."

The prologue and epilogue refer to *St. Patrick* as the first part of
a two-part drama; the second part was never written. (Part II presumably would have dealt with the conversion of a pagan king and
country to Christianity.) In the completed first part, the matter
dealing with St. Patrick has seventh-century Irish pagans concerned
about evangelical Christians, especially St. Patrick, on his way from
England. When he arrives, he converts one of King Leogarius's
courtiers, Dichu, whose sons the King condemns for their father's
apostasy. Archimagus, "the chife Priest, a Magitian," has the King
invite St. Patrick to court, where they plan to kill him. The King's
daughters, Ethne and Fedella, are ready to die with their lovers
when they hear that Ferochus and Endarius are condemned. Disguised by Archimagus as Jupiter and Mars, Ferochus and Endarius
elicit the King's promise to kill St. Patrick. The saint survives a
poison plot and revives a servant forced to drink. Leogarius's Queen
is converted; the King exiles her.

Leogarius, who had dreamt of snakes before St. Patrick arrived,
is now seeing ghosts. Archimagus promises to get rid of them if the
King will get rid of St. Patrick. The King agrees, and Archimagus
summons all the snakes in Ireland to devour St. Patrick, who drives
them out of the country. Archimagus sinks into the ground. The
saint is still suspicious of the King, but goes to court with him
anyway. The play ends with St. Patrick confiding to the converts,
"I suspect him stil; / But feare not, our good Angels still are neer
us: / Death at the last can but untie our frailty. / 'Twere happy for
our holy faith to bleed, / The Blood of Martyrs is the Churches
seed" (V.iii). The sentiment does not neutralize tragicomic resolution of the action, but it does leave the way open for a bloody sequel.

A "typical tragi-comedy" *St. Patrick* may be, but it is as entertaining a gallimaufry as any other popular tragicomedy of its time.
Contemplation of the skill with which an expert manipulates the
tools of his trade, even when the prospect affords nothing more than
a serviceable vehicle for his patrons, can suggest the pleasure and
satisfaction such a play gave Shirley's audiences. The road Caroline
theatergoers traveled in a Shirley play was well worn, but there
were always a few new points of interest along the way since it was
traveled last. In *St. Patrick* they could find a fresh shading in the

portraits of honorable lovers, elsewhere in Shirley's plays often so
rigid in their observance of what Fedella calls "form and heartless
ceremony." Ethne and Fedella discuss their suitors this way:

Ethne.   You wrong our birth and bloud,
          To think they dare neglect us, for if they
          Forget what we deserve in loving them,
          They owe more dutie, as we are the Kings
          Daughters, than to displease us so.
Fedella. That binds:
          But form and heartlesse ceremony, Sister,
          By your favor, I had rather hold my servant
          By his owne love, that chaines his heart to mine,
          Than all the bands of state. (II.i)

The exchange sounds more sophisticated than even highborn ladies
of Ireland's primitive past could manage; in a Caroline vaudeville,
it is no more inappropriate than any other anachronism. The sentiment expressed obviously mattered more for Shirley than historical
accuracy.

The most pedestrian of Shirley's efforts will carry an occasional
burst of lyricism reminiscent of the Elizabethan sonneteers, whose
excesses Shirley more than matches and sometimes renders quite
charmingly, as in the address of Corybreus, a son of King Leogarius,
to his beloved, Emeria, in the Petrarchan manner, beginning "dost
not see / As thou dost move, how every amorous plant / Doth bow
his leavy head, and beckon thee" (II.i). Again, questions of dramatic
propriety or historical authenticity are irrelevant. Here Shirley extends a simple conceit gracefully, creating an intrinsically attractive
lyric. The passage has a clear principle of organization, which the
play as a whole lacks. *St. Patrick* is a mixture, not a blend, of
inoffensively diverse elements.

VI   The Doubtful Heir

Shirley always kept in mind the audience for which he wrote.
The first prologue for *The Doubtful Heir,* originally produced in
Dublin as *Rosania, or Love's Victory,* takes account of its unusual
title and cites Suckling's *Aglaura* as a play title using a lady's name.
Shirley wants ladies to attend this play, in which wars of love are
waged, but "You fear no sigh or tear, whoever bleed; / You see, but
can take in no shot." Moreover, "Not the least rude uncivil language

shall / Approach your ear, or make one cheek look pale." The prologue for the play, after it was retitled *The Doubtful Heir* for Londoners, exhorts the audience at the Globe to try to behave as if they
were sitting in the Blackfriars.

Disdain for the common man figures fairly prominently in the
play itself, outside of the main action. The larger part of the opening
scene is given over to a series of encounters between an army captain
and two citizens, none of whom is named. The captain denounces
them at length, mainly for dunning the military. A courtier defends
city people, and the captain says that he is not attacking the class,
but only two of its least admirable members. In another army-cit-
izenry scene in the second act, the latter are returned from war and
plan to become courtiers, under the captain's guidance. In a third
encounter in the third act the humor is of a snobbish sort, cruelly
farcical. "Citizens" generally are attacked for pretension to courtliness. In the last act the two citizens the captain has "sponsored"
have lost all their money, are now cursing him, and reenlist.

The captain also appears in several of the scenes of the play's main
plot, a tragicomic action involving a claim to the throne of Murcia,
a war, imprisonment, mistaken identity and compounded disguise
(a girl dressed as a boy dressed as a girl), and a series of last-act
reversals of fortune that reconciles separated lovers. The promise
of the first prologue to ladies has been kept; the injunction in the
second prologue to ordinary playgoers has been dramatized. The
citizens in *The Doubtful Heir* may have been described as exceptions
to their class, but no nobler representatives appear.

In the main plot a claim to the throne from Prince Ferdinand
threatens the Queen of Murcia, Olivia, whose lover, Leonario,
Prince of Aragon, will fight in a war against Ferdinand. Leonario
returns in triumph, according to a courtier, Leandro, who breaks
the news in a short scene made up mainly of his two soliloquies on
the fortunes of war and on statecraft. Ferdinand is first thrown into
jail with his page, Tiberio (Rosania in disguise), and then brought
before Olivia. He does not question "Divine Providence" or the
fortunes of war, in a long speech beginning "If it be treason to be
born a Prince" and ending "If this be treason, I am guilty" (II.iv).
The speech as a whole reveals a firm command of rudimentary
rhetoric, making for better argument than dramatic verse. Olivia
spares his life; she has fallen in love with him, and they marry, but
Ferdinand does not consummate the marriage with her.

In a soliloquy Rosania-Tiberio laments Ferdinand's infidelity. Olivia enters and takes a fancy to the page. Ferdinand later assures Rosania he has not slept with Olivia. Rosania tries to get Ferdinand to perform his marital duties, so that Olivia will not ravish Tiberio. Olivia is showing Rosania-Tiberio how to make love when Ferdinand enters. When Rosania's sex is revealed, she and Ferdinand are sentenced to die. In prison again Ferdinand learns from Leandro that he, Ferdinand, is indeed the rightful king of Murcia. A series of reversals of fortune and affection in the last act leads to his assuming his kingship, a reunion with Rosania, and lasting friendship with Olivia, now united with Leonario.

Why Shirley thought the subplot might be appealing to the Dublin Irish[11] is difficult to understand, but not why the main plot would attract the English in Dublin. The mixture as before for London audiences abroad might have been just what expatriates hungry for London theater needed to satisfy their appetite. *The Doubtful Heir*, however, like the other plays Shirley wrote in Dublin, failed to attract enough English or Irish to warrant its catering to either.

CHAPTER 7

"Stranger Long to the English Scene": Plays 1640-1642

S HIRLEY spent three years and six months in Dublin from November 1636 to April 1640.[1] He returned to London as chief
dramatist for the King's men, succeeding Philip Massinger, who
died in March 1640. Within the next two years Shirley wrote four
new plays for the company, *The Imposture*, *The Cardinal* (see Chapter 8), *The Sisters*, and *The Court Secret* (not staged until after the
Restoration), his last work for the London theater. Shirley's writings
of the next twenty-four years include masques, moral allegories, and
textbooks, but no new plays.

I The Imposture

The Imposture, a tragicomedy, "had a fair reception, when it was
personated on the stage, and may march in the first rank of my own
compositions" (Dedication). Among the last of Shirley's plays, it was
the first to be staged after his return from Ireland: "He has been
stranger long to'th'English scene" (Prologue). Plague had closed the
theaters again in 1640, but only relatively briefly, for the King's
men staged *The Imposture* in November. Its "fair reception" suggests that Shirley knew how, "with artfull pen, / To charm," for artfully (according to his understanding of a poet's art[2]), if not with
inspiration, he here once again explores the character of a ruthlessly
ambitious courtier.

In the first scene Flaviano, favorite of the Duke of Mantua, makes
no secret (in soliloquy and aside) of his true nature. He works to
make "State decoyes" of "shallow Princes"; he curses when he sees
that a wounded hero, returned from battle, will live; he himself
avoids the battlefield: "he that conquers may / Get Honor, and deep

wounds, but I the day" (I.i, last lines).[3] The shocking display of villainy makes for superficially exciting theater. The monarch must beware of ambitious counselors; he must be wise enough to distinguish between the good advice of virtuous courtiers and the self-seeking counsel of such as Flaviano. Complex characterization has no place in *The Imposture:* deep-dyed villains menace simon-pure souls: "Oh, sir, you are as black, nay, have a soul / As leprous with ingratitude, as the Angels / Are white with Innocence" (Juliana, Flaviano's mistress, II.i). The cleverness with which Flaviano will be outwitted constitutes much of Shirley's "art" in arranging the parts of the play.

The opening scene of *The Imposture,* again, features tableaulike imagery, depending as it does on a great deal of personification of the kind associated with motionless figures in a masque: danger; destruction; the sun, dazzling the eyes of Mantua's besiegers; "Conquest, now hovering in the air, will mark / Her glorious perch, upon whose Plumed heads / She may advance, and clap her brazen wings" (I.i); "Victory," in the next scene, "Enamour'd on your brow / Delights to sit." And the Duke of Mantua promises to build a statue for a conquering hero, the city's deliverer, Leonato. In spite of a great deal of incident *The Imposture* has a curiously static quality, with its image of ideal court life no more disturbed by Flaviano's flamboyance than a masque would be by following it with an antimasque.

The "imposture" of the title is Juliana's, planned by Flaviano to deceive Leonato, who was promised Fioretta, the Duke's daughter. In libeling Fioretta's fiancé, Flaviano has provoked war between Mantua and Ferrara. Flaviano risks everything on his plots and pursues his aims with ever-increasing resourcefulness, creating a network of intrigue so involved that its manipulation eventually becomes impossible for him to control. Clever enough to see the trap he has made for himself, he nevertheless pursues his ends recklessly, with a certain joy when he realizes that he has reached the point of no return. There the momentum of his drive toward power is greater than his despair of reaching his goal, and he abandons his shrewdness for an irrational gamble on luck. His capacity for reasoning he has mistaken for fiat from a destiny that circumstance delayed or circumvented; he is driven to find what he believes to be his rightful place in the world, thus implicitly denying the prerogatives of birth: it is an accident that he, destined for greatness, should not be born to it. It is no accident that he ultimately surrenders himself to fate: "I have plung'd / Too farre, to hope for safety by return, / I'l trust my destiny to the stream, and reach / The point I see, or leave myself a rock / In the relentless waves" (II.i).

Shirley's victims of such intrigue as Flaviano's are often passive (contributing here to the tableaulike texture of the play), especially if they are women, and serene. These await catastrophe or a change in circumstance of any kind with an equanimity that makes the patient Griselda seem impatient by comparison. At a time when her real identity is unknown to her fiancé's sister, Fioretta responds to Donabella's sympathetic curiosity this way:

Fioretta.   When time and sorrow shall by death prepare
              My sad release of love, you may know all;
              Were the condition of my fate like others,
              It were no grief to name him.
Donabella.   This doth more inlarge my Jealousie.
Fioretta.   But let us leave this subject, till time fit
              To ope the maze of my unhappy fortune. (IV.i)

The speech is a flagrant example of an artificially created posture vis-à-vis a temporary affliction of the kind that affords Shirley's noble characters an opportunity to suffer elegantly. The created situation may thus be considered a corruption of dramatic sensibility. Pleasurable emotions, including the pain of unrequited love (pleasurably painful because the love is bound to be requited eventually), are indulged in for their own sake. Incident and character are manipulated for the sake of spurious feelings expressed in pretentious language. Such characters of Shirley's as Fioretta have no individual identity, indistinguishable as they are from play to play, except for their names. The incidents depend too much on the machinations of villains or on pure chance. True, Fioretta suffers temporarily because she has willfully sidestepped her duty, but many virtuous characters in Shirley's plays are utterly innocent of any such breach. Active or passive, or active-turned-passive, they best reveal their virtue in distress by quietly accepting whatever fate or fortune or circumstance may have in store for them.

Not entirely an innocent victim of circumstance, Fioretta had been betrothed to Leonato sight unseen and tried to escape to a nunnery when he approached Mantua to claim her. She falls in love with him as soon as she sees him. But he is in love with Juliana, who in disguise has taken Fioretta's place. Fioretta herself has come to Ferrara disguised, presumably to see Leonato for herself. She does not reveal Juliana's imposture, but admits to Donabella that she is hopelessly in love, without telling her whom she loves. In the passivity of Fioretta at this point in the plot can be seen the counterpart of Flaviano's active villainy. Arrived at an impasse, the villainous pursue their aims intrepidly; the virtuous resign themselves to fate. Whether either acts or not, both believe they are controlled by their respective destinies. Since it is the villain who continues to act at this point, it would almost seem as if to act at all were evil.

Poetic justice, however, awaits the villain Flaviano, who suffers the defection of Claudio, his "smock officer"; he is tied to a tree during a farcical scene (V.iv) built around the fool Bertoldi; but he meets his arraignment with sneering bravado (V.v). At least Flaviano remains utterly unreconstructed and does not suddenly repent (as villains in the tragicomedies often do; for example, Montalto in *The Royal Master* and Malipiero in *The Gentleman of Venice*). "Treason is sick in her short reign," declaims Leonato in the play's last couplet; "but when / Heaven sees his time, Truth takes her Throne agen." A play like *The Imposture* means to be an entertaining way of driving home the idea that the maintenance of order is of first importance in any state. Any disturbance of custom must be intrinsically evil. In a Christian monarchy any threat to order must be extirpated in the names of Heaven, Truth, and Throne, concepts treated in *The Imposture* as if they were indeed petrified.

The prologue to *The Imposture* announces that Shirley does not know the tricks to satisfy his audience: "He . . . Knowes not the mode, nor how with artfull pen / To charm." Shirley knows the tricks and knows the mode, which he goes on to disparage in the current crop of plays. Even after the theaters close, Shirley takes exception to other playwrights' work in print. In his commendatory verses to Richard Brome's *A Jovial Crew*, for example, printed in 1652 he attacks William Cartwright's recently published *Comedies, Tragi-Comedies, with Other Poems* (1651). In the early 1640s, by avoiding scurrilous language in the plays he is writing, Shirley says he seeks to please the ladies (*The Imposture*, Prologue). Their pleasure would influence "the wise," who "Will learn to like by looking on your eyes." One might wish that this prologue were written tongue-in-cheek, as the epilogue clearly was:

Juliana. Now the Play's done, I will confess to you,
      And wo'not doubt but you'll absolve me too.
      There is a mysterie, let it not go far;
      For this Confession is auricular:
      I am sent among the Nuns to fast and pray,
      And suffer piteous penance, ha, ha, ha,
      They could no better way please my desires,
      I am no Nun—but one of the Black-Friears.

The harmless joke of the boy playing Juliana is perhaps a key to the way a play like *The Imposture* may be read with understanding of authorial intention and audience expectation.

II The Sisters

The Sisters, Shirley's last play to be produced before the theaters closed September 2, 1642, reads like the libretti for operettas popular on the English stage for centuries, odd mixtures of romance, adventure, farce, and song. Frapolo, bandit chief, plans to rob the heiress Paulina, prodigal with her wealth since her father's death and scorning marriage proposals from men of her own class. She receives Lord Contarini, however, as though she were a princess at court. He falls in love with her "sweet, and humble" sister, Angellina (I.ii), who rejects his suit, saying she plans to become a nun. A troupe of "mathematicians" (astrologers and fortune-tellers: Frapolo and his band in disguise) come to Paulina's palace to steal her treasure. The banditti leave in a hurry in anticipation of an uprising, incited by Paulina's uncle, Antonio.

Angellina resists Antonio's efforts to make a "lady" out of her. Farnese, Prince of Parma, who arrives in disguise with Contarini and finds Frapolo impersonating him with Paulina, falls in love with Angellina at first sight. As in *The Gentleman of Venice*, the true parents of the proud, foolish sibling reveal her humble origin and the noble descent of her "sister": "blood will tell." The play ends with a pardon for all the banditti except Frapolo, whose punishment is that he must stay with Paulina. But in a brief epilogue Frapolo celebrates his "escape from the Prince and *Paulina*."

Such lighthearted treatment of one of Shirley's favorite themes, the affinity between natural superiority and high social rank, makes for an entertaining, if undistinguished, romantic comedy. Several indifferent plays of Shirley, however, contain interesting passages of good verse, and *The Sisters* has its share. The fourth act includes an amusing satire of Petrarchism, which features the following lines reminiscent of Shakespeare's Sonnet 130:

Angellina.   Were it not fine,
            If you should see your Mistress without hair?
            Drest only with those glittering beams you talk of?
            Two Suns instead of Eys, and they not melt
            The forhead made of Snow; no Cheeks, but two
            Roses inoculated upon a Lillie?
            Between, a pendent Alablaster Nose?
            Her Lips cut out of Corral, and no Teeth,
            But Strings of Pearl; her Tongue a Nightingales;
            Her chin a rump of Ivory, and so forth? (IV.ii)

Poetic extravagance nevertheless has a prominent place in Shirley's work—where true lovers express passion in heightened language. *The Doubtful Heir*'s straightforward lyricism ("you like the free and bounteous Sun, / Have blest me with your rayes" [IV.ii]) is often of the sort satirized in *The Sisters*. "Dost not see, / As thou dost move, how every amorous plant / Doth bow his leavy load, and beckon thee" begins an extended Petrarchan lyrical passage in *St. Patrick for Ireland* (II.i). "What a sweet thing is night" begins another in *The Constant Maid* (IV.i). The comic-operetta world of *The Sisters*, generically bizarre and fantastic, congruent in its incongruity, accomodates both satirical and straightforward treatments of Petrarchism. In such a world realistic satire and romantic lyricism may be juxtaposed no more incompatibly then solemn pronouncements on aristocratic privilege and passionate arguments for the common people's liberation from oppression. No real social conflict is explored here, for the plot works primarily to reveal Angellina's natural right by birth to the high social position illegitimately held by Paulina.

    The Sisters provides more than enough evidence needed to show that Shirley's strength and weakness as a writer for the Caroline stage depend less on his native ability than on his willingness to compromise his vision for the sake of audience approval. The overall conception of *The Sisters* becomes superficial because Shirley cannot explore its implications adequately in the context of an essentially trivial theatrical experience. Yet Shirley cleverly manipulates individual parts of the play, such as Angellina's anti-Petrarchan speech, in such a way as to suggest that he might have done better to concentrate more often and more consistently than he does on satire.

III   The Court Secret

Just as the characters in *The Court Secret* may be defined by their titles, real and assumed, so the twists and turns of the plot may be characterized as peculiar to the fictional lives of seventeenth-century aristocracy. The nobleman Piracquo has returned from exile to the court of the King of Spain, but with no assurance of safety. Maria, the Infanta, is in love with his son Manuel. Her brother Carlo is in love with Clara, daughter of the Duke Mendoza, but he is supposed to marry Isabella of Portugal, sister of Antonio, who loves Maria; Manuel loves Clara, who loves him. Roderigo, the King's brother, makes him suspicious of Piracquo and Manuel. When the King sees Antonio fighting with Manuel, he arrests Manuel, and shortly after he arrests Piracquo, too. Carlo's intercession for Piracquo leads the King to free him. The King has been "testing" Carlo's honor, as it was Carlo who arranged for Piracquo's return to Spain. But Carlo remains unhappy: he is to marry Isabella by proxy, and he still loves Clara. Carlo is ultimately revealed to be a substitute for the prince (Duke Mendoza's wife, now dead, lost the real Carlo to pirates who kidnapped the infant). Clara confirms the rumor that her suitor "Carlo" is really her brother Julio. In Manuel's cell with Clara, Maria recognizes their love and soon after agrees to marry Antonio. Piracquo confesses to kidnapping Carlo, whom he has raised as Manuel. "Manuel"-Carlo will now marry Clara; "Carlo"-Julio, Isabella; and Maria, Antonio.

Luckily, perhaps, Caroline playgoers never had to sort out the confused identities in this overwrought plot. According to the title page of the 1653 edition of *The Court Secret*, the play was "Never Acted, But prepared for the Scene at BLACK-FRIERS." One of Shirley's plays produced after the Restoration, *The Court Secret* adds nothing to what the dramatist had offered in earlier tragicomedies. Worthy courtiers struggle to maintain their integrity; several young lovers play musical chairs with their alliances for four acts before their proper matching in the last; a courtier's wife was responsible for the problems created before the action of the play begins; solutions reveal that the finest young man, the most courageous, the man most desired by the ladies of the court, has the noblest blood, thereby demonstrating, as his male and female counterparts in *The Gentleman of Venice* and *The Sisters*, respectively, do, the natural superiority of the highborn.

The date of the play, 1642, invites speculation about its relevance to current affairs of state in England, because of the prominence in the play of terms like "whisper," "secrecy," and "mystery," and such observations as "it is hard to say when men / Dissemble not at Court" (I.i). When Shirley has an unnamed courtier say "we are / Not sure of anything at Court" (II.i), he is indirectly either complimenting the English court or warning it against tyranny: only foreign princes abuse their power. Any prince's brow, however, can change without warning. His "frown" frightens, and his "royal beam" brightens. His favor should be bestowed on those who will not betray his confidence. The stricture would appear to apply to all courts, not just to the English. Shirley dedicated the play in 1653 to the son of Thomas Strafford, whom he had known in Ireland. The "poem . . . happened to receive birth, when the Stage was interdicted" (Dedication). Shirley does not mention the elder Strafford. Since he wrote *The Court Secret* in 1642, he cannot have designed it with a view to saving Strafford, whose enemies at court and in Parliament, not Charles, were responsible for his arrest and execution in 1641. The dedication, then, should not suggest a more specific reference to English court affairs than Shirley's fictional treatment, in *The Court Secret* and elsewhere, of his favorite themes.

CHAPTER 8

"Seeds of Honour": The Lady of Pleasure *and* The Cardinal

S HIRLEY is best known for two plays: a comedy, *The Lady of Pleasure*, and a tragedy, *The Cardinal* (often referred to as the last great tragedy of the English Renaissance). Although *The Lady of Pleasure* appears in the middle of Shirley's career and *The Cardinal* at the end, each represents in unique ways the culmination of Shirley's efforts in their respective genres. *The Lady of Pleasure* deserves its reputation as a brilliant comedy of manners; *The Cardinal* has more historical interest than intrinsic artistic merit: Shirley's forte was comedy. In the tragedies and tragicomedies his moral-didactic strain makes noble heroes and heroines often sound like mouthpieces for Royalist propaganda; for the comedies' satire it provides a reasonable standard of judgment.

I The Lady of Pleasure

Lady Aretina Bornwell, newly arrived in London from the country, thoroughly enjoys city pleasures, and disparages rural entertainments. Her steward, a country gentleman, displeases her by recalling the peace and harmony she has left behind. Sir Thomas Bornwell, too, deplores the exchange of "a calme and retire[d] life / For this wild towne, compos'd of noise and charge" (I.i). A brief, whirlwind appearance by a busy lady-about-town, Decoy, to arrange a dinner engagement with Lady Aretina would seem to confirm Sir Thomas's impression of his wife's involvement in a giddy social whirl.[1] The longer visit of two young gallants, Alexander Kickshaw and John Littleworth, bursting with town gossip, leads him to take

drastic measures: he will pretend to abandon his temperate ways
for the pursuit of pleasure.

The opening scene of *The Lady of Pleasure* avoids sinking into
solemnity or evaporating into triviality by moving briskly between
the steward's and Sir Thomas's admonitions and the other characters'
light-headed utterances. Aretina leaves the scene briefly to fuss with
her hair: "here's a curle / Straddle[s] most impiously," while Sir
Thomas manages to hold his own with Kickshaw and Littleworth.
"I see the folly of my thrift," he tells them, "and will / Repent in
sacke and prodigalitie," proceeding to list the amusements he will
enjoy. "Hee's exalted," exclaims Kickshaw approvingly. In addition
to the rapid movement of the scene, the skillful manipulation of the
play's key terms, "pleasure" and "honour" or their equivalents,
creates a verbal texture that maintains a delicate balance between
moral concern and urbane satire here and throughout the play.

The second scene introduces Lady Celestina Bellamour, described in the first scene as a rich sixteen-year-old widow, and her
steward, who is concerned about his mistress's extravagance, gre-
gariousness, and most of all her reputation. The structural parallel
extends to a visit from an as yet dimly perceived character, Haircut
(who presents himself as a courtier and proposes marriage to Celestina), to be followed by one from two relatives, Lady Novice and
her sister, Celestina's "pupils," to whom she plans to "read . . .
Court Philosophie" (I.ii). The steward's admonitions are kept to a
minimum, and the young widow's brash assertiveness is leavened
like Aretina's by wit. Celestina deals confidently with Haircut: "How
long doe you imagine you can love sir? / Is it a Quotidian, or will it
hold / But every other day?" The second scene, clearly a variation of
the first, again builds its argument on the honor-pleasure conflict:
"Must I be limited to please your honour?" Celestina demands of
her steward, "Or for the vulgar breath confine my pleasures."

The second act like the first moves from the Bornwell residence
to Celestina's. At Bornwell's the action exploits the comic aspect of
Aretina's fashionable posture. Appalled by her nephew Frederick's
unpolished academic manner, she threatens to faint when he refers
to his studies, for "he did name / Logicke, and may for aught I know,
be gone / So farre to understand it" (II.i). To please his aunt, Fred
erick bids farewell to Aristotle and proceeds to study the "arts of
London." At Celestina's her friends Mariana and Isabella admire
the "art worthy a Ladies practise" (II.ii), with which Celestina will
enjoy courtship and avoid "new marriage fetters": "pleasures with

a security of our honour," as the young widow puts it. Celestina's suitors, Haircut again and a new one, Sir William Scentlove, provide an occasion for exercise of her wit, which takes the edge off her apparently callous plans: she describes Haircut as "the sweetest of all men that visit me. . . . He is full of powder, / He will save much in perfume for my chamber, / Were he but constant here." When she meets her neighbor Bornwell for the first time, she quickly and easily recognizes a fellow spirit. Celestina sees through Bornwell's rakish behavior, as her other guests do not; she was already familiar with the Bornwells' respective reputations (their "several merits"). The parallel situations and characters of the first two acts converge with Bornwell and Celestina's meeting, and Celestina's orientation to London society is clearly distinguished from Aretina's. The understanding between Bornwell and Celestina, with both joining her other guests in a dance that concludes the scene, foreshadows the last-act reconciliation, again in dance, of honor and pleasure.

In the third act the scene shifts to Lord A.'s residence, where Haircut functions as a barber and Decoy as a bawd. Lord A., mourning the death of Bella Maria, rejects Decoy's offer of a liaison with his cousin Aretina. His dead love's miniature Kickshaw and Scentlove compare unfavorably to Celestina, whom Lord A. agrees to meet. The scene is designed to reflect the play's theme of honor and pleasure in Lord A.'s ambiguous moral position: he interrupts dictation of a letter warning Aretina about Decoy's untrustworthiness to listen to Kickshaw and Scentlove's silly chatter.

At Bornwell's Aretina takes center stage. The busy, crowded second scene of the third act focuses on her maneuverings, the ploys attendant on a campaign to dominate a politely corrupt milieu. Now aware, thanks to Lord A., of Decoy's function in high society, Aretina uses her to advance a plot. She recruits Littleworth and Kickshaw to defame Celestina; she gets the better of Celestina in an exchange of compliments (in French), at least to the point where the younger, prettier woman retires gracefully from the fray. Aretina seems to be in complete control of her ménage until the arrival of Frederick, the erstwhile sober scholar now offensively, not fashionably, drunk, lecherous, and pugnacious. And her plot against Celestina fails: the clever girl proves to be more than a match for Littleworth and Kickshaw. At the end of the scene Aretina is still plotting intrigues, but not without misgivings: "I blush while I converse with my owne thoughts, / Some strange fate governs me, but I must on, / The wayes are cast already, and we thrive / When our sinne feares no eye nor perspective" (III.ii).

The fourth act has three settings: at Decoy's, Bornwell's, and Celestina's. The first scene is farcical (Decoy disguised as an ugly old hag luring Kickshaw into her bed). The second scene is mostly satiric (the target foppery, as Frederick displays his fancy new clothes to the Bornwell steward and Littleworth), but moves, as the second scene of the third act does, toward a crisis of confidence in the strategies adopted by the leading characters in the play: Aretina acknowledges to her husband the excellence of Celestine's attributes and wonders how any man could resist her; Bornwell, alone, wonders if his mock-flirtation with Celestina might not disguise his attraction to her. The third scene is seriocomic, the first encounter between Celestina and Lord A., conducted with civility, wit, and caution. The conduct of the action in the fourth act as a whole contrives to suspend resolution of a trio of romantic intrigues and to sharpen perception of each as an honorable or dishonorable search for gratification: Kickshaw does not know what his fear and greed will lead to, as he submits to Decoy's blandishments; the Bornwells flounder temporarily as they struggle with their respective desires, Aretina's to glitter in high society, Sir Thomas's to resist temptation; Celestina and Lord A., strongly attracted to each other, part mutually dissatisfied. Promiscuity in the first scene, marital infidelity in the second, and misunderstanding in the third threaten the characters involved, the threats arising as much from the way of their world as from their respective capacities for honorable conduct.

The last act, presented as a single scene, is actually made up of three distinct parts, the first and third flanking another encounter between Celestina and Lord A., in which the lovers form an honorable alliance. The first part brings Aretina to an understanding of her follies; the last reconciles a repentant wife and husband. Cellestina and Lord A. come to an understanding on stage; the Bornwells, off stage.[2] The fifth-act setting returns the action to Bornwell's house, with the master behaving as irresponsibly as Aretina in the first act. He is playing the part of a roistering rake as he continues to cater to Aretina's image of a London gentleman casually indulging in wine, women, and song. Aretina disguises her concern by proposing expenditures as extravagant as his and by lightheartedly dismissing the prospect of bankruptcy within a month. She is further troubled here by her dealings with Decoy, Kickshaw, and Frederick, now so unrestrained as to make romantic overtures to his aunt.

Before the act is over, Aretina, in addition to reforming herself, has persuaded Frederick to return to college and is resolved to reform Decoy and Kickshaw. Choice of setting, disposition of action, and character development in the last act of *The Lady of Pleasure* insist upon the social ramifications of personal conflicts between honor and pleasure.

References to honor outnumber those to pleasure, and to related terms such as delight and entertainment, in the play as a whole. *Pleasure* and *honor* are frequently juxtaposed, as in Kickshaw's greeting to Arentina, "Pleasures attend you Madam, / How does my plant of honour?" (IV.ii). By the time honor and pleasure are no longer in conflict, no insistence upon their compatibility is necessary. The form that honorable pleasure assumes expresses that sentiment eloquently: "musicke," orders Sir Thomas Bornwell in the concluding speech of *The Lady of Pleasure*; "and when our Ladies / Are tired with active motion, to give / Them rest in some new rapture to advance / Full mirth, our soules shall leape into a dance" (V.i). |

The "leap" will effect a precipitate transition from physical activity to an elegant movement of the soul, one that gives pleasure of a different sort from the kind Sir Thomas's lady has pursued since her arrival in London. The play's last lines recall the first: "Be patient Madam; you may have your pleasure" (Steward to Aretina, I.i). On her arrival in London Aretina abjured "the countrey conversation"; now the Bornwells will return to a rural life, as soon as they have entertained, and been entertained by, Celestina, an adept at city ways and genuinely gracious living. The latter and Lord A. wax lyrically and at length on the pleasures of a rural romance: "Consent to be my Mistris *Celestina*, / And we will have it Spring-time all the yeare," Lord A. woos her (V.i). After a catalogue of pleasures to be proved, if she will come live with him, Celestina parodies it with a list of her own. Lord A. responds: "You chide me hansomely, pray tell me how, / You like this language." Celestina begs, "Good my Lord forbeare," and he does. Their relationship will henceforth be conducted on a social level and in a language appropriate to their station in life. Celestina reminds him of his ancestry—and of her honor, neither of which may be bought "for price of gold, or pleasure."

Honor is the music to which a dramatist's soul dances in *The Lady of Pleasure*. Variations on the theme of honor here define character and determine the direction of the play's action; yet for all its frequency, the term is never once used without careful attention to the immediate dramatic context. When Aretina impatiently seeks to enter the fashionable life, her indulgent husband wonders at her anger. "I am angry with my selfe," she says, "To be so miserably restrained in things, / Wherein it doth concerne your love and honour / To see me satisfied" (I.i). Her concept of a husband's honor marks her as unthinking and irresponsible; his indulgence of her misconception leads her into a series of near-dishonorable encounters with a variety of unsavory Londoners; and him, as a countermeasure to bring her around to a mature sense of honor, into prodigality and dalliance she ultimately will not be able to countenance.

The honorable Bornwell deliberately outdoes his fun-loving lady in a hectic pursuit of pleasure. But first he tries to reason her out of her mindless excesses: "Something might here be spar'd, [with safety] of / Your birth and honour, since the truest wealth / Shines from the soul, and draws up just admirers" (I.i). The first chords of the play's music have been struck; honor has first been associated with love; to Aretina at this point "honour" is synonymous with "condition" (status, social position). Mildly rebuked for abandoning "a calme and retired life" for one "compos'd of noise and charge," she asks, "What charge more than is necessarie / For a Lady of my birth and education?" Bornwell first associates honor with birth in the second act, and shortly after he brings together all three terms, honor, birth, and education: "Learning is an addition beyond / Nobilitie of birth, honour of blood / Without the ornament of knowledge, is / A glorious ignorance" (II.i).

At the beginning of the play Bornwell had related "honour" to income, defending himself against an implied charge of parsimony with "my poorest servant / Shall not upbraid my tables, nor his hire / Purchasd beneath my honour" (I.i). To Aretina's charge that reticence about displaying one's wealth means unpopularity, Bornwell had responded, "I have / No great ambition to buy preferment / At so deare rate," countered by Aretina's "Nor I to sell my honour, / By living poore and sparingly." An argument between Celestina and her steward first deals with honor in relation to the cost of her wardrobe: "Must I be limited to please your honour?" asks Celestina before she strikes him (I.ii). Aretina's steward advises her studious nephew Frederick, who has abandoned, at his aunt's request, the university for the city, "you shall / Want nothing, if you can be proud, and spend it / For my Ladies honour" (II.i). Frederick will "do honor" to his aunt—will add to her reputation—not by wearing scholar's black or by speaking Latin or by learning logic, but by spending a lot of money.

The term *honour* appears no fewer than sixty-five times in the play and twice in Shirley's brief dedication of the play to Lovelace. With respect to the pleasures the privileged members of society might reasonably enjoy, honor translated into honorable action involved, for Shirley, a strict observance of the rules governing their behavior. The highest classes share with the lowest responsibility for conducting themselves in a manner that becomes their station in life. The ungainly plowman dancing a morris might invite an unreconstructed Aretina's outright scorn, but it has its place for her astute gentleman-steward in "country life" as "the pleasure of a kingdome" (I.i). The soul-dance of the plowman's superior, whose will commands "what should move / Delights"—Aretina's "husbands love and power joyned," her steward reminds her, give their life "more harmony"—is more exacting even than the "active motion" of which the ladies will tire: the harmonious motion of the kingdom's best hearts and minds, moving gracefully to the music of honor.

II   The Cardinal

Some of the scholarly interest in *The Cardinal* arises from its supposed historical and biographical parallels. Shirley's cryptic Prologue does suggest ("keep your fancy active," "Think what you please") and almost simultaneously disowns (" 'tis nothing so," "I will say nothing positive") a parallel between the characters of the play and contemporary public figures. The "shorthaird men" about whom the Duchess Rosaura warns the Cardinal (II.iii), in an attempt to get him to change his high-handed ways, may very well be Spanish counterparts of the Roundheads, the English Puritans critical of the Anglican Church in the 1630s and 1640s. But there is no other internal evidence of the play's alleged topicality or occasional intent. Rather, *The Cardinal* represents Shirley's last attempt to write a great play in the revenge-tragedy tradition; its setting and action were possibly suggested by John Webster's *The Duchess of Malfi*.

The atmosphere of the royal court in *The Cardinal* is dangerous. Discretion and caution guide discussion of court affairs, as in the opening scene, where two unnamed lords deliver most of the exposition. The powerful have spies everywhere ("Take heed, the Cardinal holds Intelligence / With every bird i'th'air"), near the beginning of the play; near the end, "But do not talk too loud, we are

not all / Honest i' the house, some are the Cardinals creatures" (V.ii).
The King enjoys absolute sovereignty, which cannot be disputed.
The King's favorite, the Cardinal, exercises his will unchecked
("Death on his purple pride, / He governs all" [I.i]).

The immediate issue in the first scene is the widowed Duchess
Rosaura's impending marriage to the Cardinal's nephew, Columbo,
although she loves the Count d'Alvarez. Alvarez and Rosaura are
ideally suited to each other (*"Hymen* cannot tie / A knot of two more
equall hearts and blood"), but the wise and honorable Alvarez has
deferred to the Cardinal's, and thus the King's, wishes through
"Wisdom," not "Fear." In the wayward currents of court life dominated by such a powerful intriguer as the Cardinal, noble souls
struggle to steer straight in an honorable direction. Images of stream,
storm, and wind in the opening scene of *The Cardinal* insist upon
the turbulent nature of the King of Navarre's court and upon the
heroic effort required to maintain integrity in an unstable atmosphere.

The second scene, with attunements to female sensibility peculiar
to Shirley, presents a paragon of courtly grace whose physical beauty
is an essential attribute. On her first appearance in the play the
Duchess Rosaura is addressed by one of her ladies-in-waiting as
"the noblest frame / Of beauty that this Kingdom ever boasted" (I.ii).
Rosaura's state of mind, which affects her appearance unfavorably,
causes concern for her painful adjustment to widowhood. Rosaura
is still mourning her late husband, while her attendants would have
her anticipating a second marriage joyfully, in accord with her "New
dress, and smiling garment." Rosaura resolves to create an un-
troubled appearance for the court, with the proviso that ladies-in-
waiting Valeria and Celinda do not mention her grief or advise her
to forget it. Not fear or awe, but deference to superior sensibility
dictates the caution with which noble men and women sometimes
share intimate confidences with royalty. Valeria asks permission of
Rosaura to be bold; Rosaura bids her speak freely. Such freedom
is a sign of favor, and at their best those closest to majesty recognize
the special privilege they enjoy at the pleasure of their superiors.

After she has listened to Valeria and Celinda's frank opinions,
which she had solicited and licensed, Rosaura, alone, complains of
the constraints on her own freedom. What good does it do her to
be "born above these Ladies"? She has not the greatness of the
King; she is, paradoxically, enslaved by her greatness; Valeria and
Celinda are free to love whom they choose, she says. Of course, in

several plays, characters like Rosaura or her King often arrange marriages for women like Valeria and Celinda; marriage to men they love would appear to be a happy accident. Shirley does not hint at irony in his depiction of Rosaura's sentiments here; her pity for herself should be shared by his audience. Perhaps Rosaura's unwillingness to confide in Valeria and Celinda entitles her to sympathy; what she really thinks and feels she keeps to herself. She struggles to behave like a duchess and to be true, at the same time, to herself. She will muster her courage, "assume / The privilege I was born with," and tell the King that "he hath no power nor art / To steer a Lovers Soul."

Antonio, her secretary, whom she had sent to Alvarez, tells her he is waiting to see her, and also advises her of an impending war. Rosaura's hopes rise. Antonio's news gives her some reason for thinking there is a way out of the arranged marriage to Columbo, for the Cardinal's nephew is to lead the troops of Navarre against Aragon. She wishes him dead, but orders Antonio not to tell anyone what she has said. Antonio predicts that Columbo's scheduled departure will bring him quickly to Rosaura, and he leaves. Rosaura, again alone, impatient to say goodbye to Columbo, rejoins Valeria and Celinda, who have been talking to each other apart. They welcome her smiles, genuine this time, although they do not suspect their sinister cause. Rosaura's elation here represents a perversion of noble sentiment. She is now rather enjoying her need to conceal her true feelings.

Valeria and Celinda opened the second scene with remarks about Rosaura's appearance; first genuinely sad, she later pretends to be cheerful, then positively gleeful, but not for the reason her ladies-in-waiting think she is. Now Rosaura remarks on Columbo's happiness. And he is genuinely happy to have been appointed general of the army. He will win his victory before he marries Rosaura. Columbo feels exactly the way he says he does. He is aware, from the indulgent smiles of Valeria and Celinda, that his attempt at courtly address to Rosaura reveals that he is no adept at "Court tacticks." Rosaura tells him that the King is cruel to separate them and to risk Columbo's life. Columbo replies that the opportunity to fight is a greater gift than Rosaura's beauty. Antonio reenters to announce the King and the Cardinal. The King promises a splendid marriage on Columbo's return; the Cardinal approves of Rosaura's "sadness" at parting from Columbo. Rosaura bids farewell to the general, who leaves with the King, the Cardinal, and several lords.

She dismisses Valeria and Celinda. For the third time alone on stage, she is not conscience-stricken by her dissimulation, for she is being true to Alvarez, to whom she pledged her love: "Forgive me virtue that I have dissembled, / And witness with me, I have not a thought / To tempt or to betray him, but secure / The promise I first made to love and honour" (I.ii). Antonio enters to announce Alvarez. Alone again for a moment, Rosaura wonders how she ought to behave.

Her ladies-in-waiting, still unmarried, are not yet answered for. Valeria's shift of preference from Alvarez to Columbo indicates the latter's superior attractiveness, not capriciousness in her. Rosaura loves Alvarez and has pledged herself to him; honor in love makes it impossible for her to obey the King and accept Columbo. Alvarez is ready to obey Rosaura's commands, but she will not command where she once promised love. She reminds him of the sacredness of their "mutual vows"—perhaps he doubts his own faith? But he takes orders from the King, and he urges Rosaura not to let him be a millstone round her neck. She must "Preserve [her] greatness." Rosaura deplores her higher station and insists that Alvarez's blood is as noble as that of kings. He reminds her that there are other considerations, such as the King's displeasure if they should not obey. A threat arises from the Cardinal's "Plot to advance" Columbo, himself no one to be trifled with. Any of them or all three could ruin Alvarez and Rosaura. She wants to know if Alvarez is afraid. He is, but only for her. He is ready to suffer; his "single tragedy" would be minor, for he is so much beneath her. Rosaura wants to know what he would do if Columbo should die in battle or give her up. It would be like heaven, he says. But he has reconciled himself to losing her, and he leaves. Alone again, Rosaura resolves to have Alvarez, one way or another. Honor and concern for Rosaura lead Alvarez to accept, however reluctantly, the impediment to fulfillment of their love. Honor in love leads Rosaura to choose her contrary course of action. She is not a passive heroine.

Meanwhile, Columbo is pleased with the morale of his military council outside the town taken by the Aragonians, who have not destroyed the wealthy city in the course of helping themselves to everything there they wanted. Colonel Hernando of Columbo's army advises a waiting period, until the army of occupation becomes soft. A "First Colonel" disagrees. Waiting means fear, conquest increases courage, and news of the success of Aragon will attract more men to its army. Hernando points out that the Navarre army is smaller and untrained; Alphonso puts his faith in the men's spirit. Columbo accuses Hernando of cowardice or treason; Hernando resigns. Alphonso and the First Colonel reassure Hernando that he is valiant. Columbo sends him with a letter to the King saying that Columbo is going to attack: "A pretty Court way / Of dismissing an Officer" (II.i), according to Hernando. Hernando leaves; Columbo challenges those who remain to risk death and to ask the same of their men. He has a plan of action for that night. Antonio enters with letters from Rosaura, asking for her release from their engagement. Columbo is deeply insulted and draws a pistol to kill Antonio, who tells him Rosaura did not look angry when she gave him the letter. Columbo now thinks Rosaura wants him to test her, so he answers her letter "Beyond her expectation" to "put / Her soul to a noble test." Antonio congratulates himself, in an aside, on getting out of a difficult situation. His description of Rosaura's manner when she gave him the letter has led Columbo to believe that she is testing *him*. Inexperienced as a courtier, the soldierly Columbo confidently believes that "Love has a thousand arts." While he writes, his officers discuss the loyalty of his men, his prospective marriage, and the early demise of Rosaura's first husband, who left her a virgin (they had been married before either of them was old enough to consummate the marriage). Columbo gives Antonio his reply and sends his officers to their posts.

His uncle, the Cardinal, intends to visit Rosaura daily during Columbo's absence. Rosaura apologizes for her inability to entertain him as he deserves. The Cardinal assures her of his favor. The two politely exchange compliments, but, in the light of Rosaura's earlier revelation of her true feelings and intentions, her references to his power can be understood as at least ironic. The Cardinal takes them as evidence of her bounteous nobility. Alone once again, Rosaura admits she is playing a dangerous game. She dare not anger the Cardinal until she knows how Columbo reacts to her letter. She trusts that the "greatness of his soul" will not allow him to take a wife who "comes with murmur," (II.ii), that is, with reservations, demurrers—if he understands her letter. Antonio returns with Columbo's reply. Rosaura does not realize that Columbo thinks he is playing her game of testing, and joy replaces her fear. She rewards Antonio and leaves, saying, "*Columbo* now is noble."

The King attributes the breach between Columbo and Hernando to Columbo's quick temper, which subsides as quickly as it flares up. He orders Hernando to return to the front. Two lords advise

Hernando not to submit and to wait until Columbo discovers his error in dismissing him. They warn him to beware the Cardinal's plots, which he says do not bother him. His loyalty to the King cannot be shaken. He means to obey the command to return. Alvarez admits to the King that Rosaura and he have been in love, but that now he defers to her honor and to the King's election. When Rosaura shows the King Columbo's letter, he consents to her marrying Alvarez. The Cardinal is puzzled and angry, chastising Rosaura for rushing to a meaner man. They exchange rather harsh words, she accusing him of partiality, he her of "licence"—and Alvarez of "effeminacy." Rosaura defies him; he plans "action and revenge" to "calm her fury" (II.iii).

Valeria and Celinda are puzzled by Columbo's release of Rosaura, the more so when they learn of his victory and imminent return to court. They leave on the entrance of the Cardinal, who is discontented about the marriage of Rosaura and Alvarez. He cannot understand what Columbo has done. In the next scene he does, when Columbo clarifies his behavior, bloodily. A "company of Cavaliers" led by Columbo, all masked, invite Alvarez off stage. The masquers return with the dead body of Alvarez and leave, except for Columbo, who removes his mask. Rosaura demands justice, and the King promises her she shall have it. A servant enters to report the masquers' flight. Columbo gives Rosaura's letter to the King, who appears to be looking for a way to exonerate the murderer but is still angry with him for killing Alvarez in his presence. Columbo pleads his record of service, displeasing the King with rash remarks about dependence on soldiers in crisis and neglect in peacetime. The King orders him arrested. Columbo is guilty of a breach of etiquette (*lèse-majesté*) in displaying Alvarez's corpse in the royal presence. Not the murder, but the manner, arouses the King's greater displeasure.

Later, Hernando and others wonder at Columbo's exoneration, and they broach the possibility of a resumption of negotiations for marriage to Rosaura. Hernando, meaning to kill the Cardinal, goes to consult with Rosaura. Also on his way to see her is the Cardinal himself, whom the King is sending to comfort her. Rosaura is determined to get revenge. To carry out her plan, she feigns madness. The Cardinal will not kill her while she is mad, for then she would not suffer the full force of his punishment. He means to rape and poison her. In the last act, dialogue between Rosaura and Hernando makes it intriguingly difficult to tell whether or not she is really mad. Certainly Hernando thinks so. When the Cardinal begins his sexual assault on her, he finds, with his first kiss, that he is falling in love with her. She calls for help. Hernando rushes in to kill the Cardinal. Rosaura leaves; Antonio rouses the court; he recognizes Hernando, who kills himself; the King, Rosaura, Valeria, and various lords and guards enter; Hernando dies;[3] Rosaura appears to have recovered her wits; the Cardinal begs mercy and warns Rosaura that she is poisoned; he offers an antidote, which is actually poison; Rosaura drinks it; he reveals his duplicity and dies; Rosaura dies.

The action of *The Cardinal* is rendered in a style best described in relation to a distinctive pattern of imagery, a contained imagery developed by pervasive reference to the color cardinal. "I would have't a Comedie, / For all the purple in the name," says Shirley in the prologue, and, he might have added, for all the purple in the play. In the first act an anonymous lord at the court of the King of Navarre takes the first step on the purple path of *The Cardinal* by cursing the title character with "Death on his purple pride" (I.i). Columbo postpones his wedding for a war, "the purple field of glory" (I.ii). Elsewhere the Cardinal or his dress are referred to in such expressions as "the purple gownman" and "Your reverend purples," while the reference to his nephew ("his soul is purpled o'er") links the Cardinal imagery directly to references to "blood" (in its various meanings), to "bloody," and to "bleeding": "I would not shrink to bleed," "envious blood," "The gloss of blood and merit," "partial where your blood runs," "innocence must bleed," "cool bloods," "a common man, whose blood has no / Ingredient of honour," vindication of Columbo's honor that "might have been / Less bloody," "guilt of blood," "Alvarez' blood," and twenty-two other "bloody" phrases, not to mention related terms: "Ambition and scarlet sins," "holy blushes," "the Church's wounds," "crimson penitence," "red eyes," "weeping wounds," "arteries," and "guilty flowings"; the Cardinal described as a "red cock"; "hot veins," and a dozen more references to "wound," "blush," and "scarlet." The iteration makes for a consistent but monochromatic verbal texture. One need not prefer Webster's more diffusely colored image patterns, with their affinity to the excesses of his sensational plots, to find Shirley's design less evocative than it is "neat."

The coolness, even cold-bloodedness, of Shirley's distancing from the action of *The Cardinal* neutralizes passionate conflict, much as the King's abstract, all-embracing moral comment at the end on the resolution of that conflict neutralizes the horror of the mutual destruction of all the leading characters. The nobility of Rosaura, Columbo, and Hernando becomes a reflection of a fixed attitude toward birth and honor, not a nobility experienced. The depravity of the Cardinal, culminating in an attempted rape and a successful poisoning, becomes an aberration, not a consequence of a highborn churchman's preoccupation with family pride, reputation, and political power. *The Cardinal*, like many of Shirley's plays, is artfully structured, but unlike several, lifeless and essentially undramatic. Yet Shirley considered *The Cardinal* his best play (Dedication). In the prologue he moderates his judgment to "this play / Might rival with his best." Some commentators on *The Cardinal* have agreed with him.[4]

CHAPTER 9

"A Poem for the Scene": Evaluation and Reevaluation

CAROLINE conventions, theatrical and social, and the dramatic genres to which his plays belong determine the character of Shirley's works, individually and as a whole, more distinctly than any unique features of style. Most of Shirley's heroes and heroines lack the complexity of Webster's or Ford's. They are, in fact, interchangeable from play to play. Whole speeches (except for direct reference to specific characters or action) can be transferred from Catalina (or Berinthia) in *The Maid's Revenge* to Rosaura in *The Cardinal* without violating the latter's characterization. Such substitution would be impossible for Webster's Vittoria in *The White Devil* and the Duchess of Malfi, for Ford's Calantha in *The Broken Heart* and Annabella in *'Tis Pity She's a Whore*—or for Shirley's own Clariana in *Love's Cruelty* and any other of his heroines. On those occasions when imaginative identification with individual characters produces psychologically sound utterance, Shirley avoids the undifferentiated declamation that too often marks the speech of his aristocratic characters. Most of his major figures are better designated as figureheads, products of the kind of nominal characterization by type associated with the morality plays of the fifteenth century.

The differentiation among types according to social class accounts for the simplistic characterization of the major figures in Shirley's tragedies and tragicomedies, always excepting *Love's Cruelty*. Strict observance of the rules of propriety governing the stage presentation of Cavalier and commoner alike suggests that Shirley subscribed wholeheartedly to the idea that "blood will tell." In *The Gentleman of Venice*, where the natural worth of a gardener appears to discount the belief that breeding determines character, the commoner is revealed to be a changeling, a man of noble birth substituted in infancy for a servant's child. Juxtaposition of baseness and nobility in *The Traitor* has a servant describing his master's declining health (he is wasting away for love) and claiming that "nere a woman in the world should make / Me hang my selfe" (I.i).[1] In spite of the injunction "Always beware of the extreemes" (Cosmo to Oriana, *The Traitor*, II.ii), idealized courtiers cannot avoid them: moral strength of the kind dramatized in *The Traitor* requires them to make heroic life-or-death commitments, as the violent action that resolves crucial problems indicates. The nobility of Shirley's noble ladies and gentlemen is enhanced by contrast with the baseness of lower-class characters.

Shirley's depiction of the military most clearly illustrates his method of characterization by class. Between the commoner and the nobleman is the soldier, who may belong to either of their classes. The good soldier is a man of virtuous and courageous action who has no use for fancy talk. Colonel Conquest in *Honoria and Mammon* eschews elegant language: "I have / No stock of perfum'd words" (I.ii).[2] Captain Conquest represents an ideal; obviously all military men are not as honorable as he. Aurelio Andreozzi and Pisauro in *The Opportunity* are gentlemen in financial straits, off to war to repair their fortunes; an unexpected access of wealth (when a Duchess seems to be favoring Aurelio) would eliminate the need to become soldiers, says Pisauro: "If the Dutchesse should be in love with him, / Here were a purchase, I doe verily / Beleeve here will be an end of all our warres, / If he have but the grace to march upon / This service and charge home" (I.ii). But professional soldiers, though they may be involved in plots either on the hero's or the villain's side, receive preferential treatment from Shirley. Captain Aquinas in *The Politician* is no traitor, as he appears to be, but loyal to his commander, who says of him, "Although *Gotharus* had contriv'd my ruine, / 'Twas counterplotted by this honest Captaine" (V.ii).

In judgment of the military Shirley observes as strict a standard of excellence as of any other division of society. In *The Young Admiral* the thoughtful military man is superior to the simpleminded, and the courageous soldier is superior to the ungrateful citizen, none too surprisingly. Military life receives a good deal of attention in *The Young Admiral*, with some of the details quite uncompromisingly graphic. Two servants' discussion of the officer class, in a fairly long comic scene at the beginning of the third act, includes

grisly pictures of battle casualties and atrocities. The exchange between two minor characters contrasts strikingly with abstract
speeches about "honor" elsewhere in the play. As low on the scale
of honor as the cowardly soldier or servant class is the courtier who
has nothing to do with soldiers in peacetime. Captain Mauricio
speaks contemptuously to the nobleman Fabio, who comes to him
for protection when Naples is under siege (*The Young Admiral*,
III.ii). Yet Mauricio will protect Fabio for half the nobleman's property, payable only if the captain survives the battle. The agreement
points up the financial plight of the underpaid military.[3] The commoner tries to avoid military duty; the common soldier fights for
pay; the gentlemanly soldier willingly risks his life for honor.
Shirley's characterization of soldiers extends the popular image of
the class to conform to his aristocratic ideal. The range of characterization remains limited, without penetration beyond the bound-
aries of type.

Shirley belongs in the company of writers with a flair for theater
who can be relied on by producers to turn out serviceable vehicles
for their companies, but who rarely create great drama. Like most
of the professional dramatists of the 1620s, 1630s, and 1640s, Shirley
wrote to order. Throughout his career he sustained a quite respectable level of composition and sometimes even achieved the kind of
ripeness that he spoke of in the prologue to his "first fruits." However hackneyed and complicated his plots (and however lacking in
complexity), however dogmatic his convictions, however superficial
his characterizations (with a few notable exceptions), his work
pleased the audiences for whom it was designed. For them he was
stylish, glib, mannered, funny,[4] sensational,[5] sentimental, and inoffensively moralistic.

Straightforward moralizing in Shirley's plays expresses no more
and no less than might be expected from the conventionally virtuous
characters who are its vehicles. Shirley's uncluttered thinking has
a distinct advantage for the theater: the playwright can devote his
attention to fashioning clear-cut confrontations immediately stim-
ulating on stage, such as that involving a secret concealed from a
sympathetic character (but known to the audience). As much because of his aesthetic convictions as for the sake of theatrical effectiveness, Shirley works for simplicity of expression and clarity in
characterization. Consequently his characters tend to lack psychological complexity, and his language shows little irony and attendant
subtlety. Among Shirley's contemporaries John Ford is the most

likely candidate for tortured questioning of traditional morality.
Ford's characters' moral pronouncements flash ironically in context,
whereas Shirley's recall the unlarded, undramatic aphorisms of the
interludes and early Elizabethan plays.

Shirley's sense of conflict is constricted by unconstrained accep-
tance of moral absolutes. Only in *Love's Cruelty* does his perspective
widen enough to permit glimpses into terrifying abysses of nihilism
that make *King Lear, The Duchess of Malfi, The Revenger's Tragedy*, and *The Broken Heart* fascinating, where the tension between
vision and medium creates dramatic ambivalences infinitely more
demanding of language than Shirley's generally calm periods. Superficially similar in construction to the tragedy *The Maid's Revenge*,
which begins as a romantic comedy, and to the tragicomedy *The
Wedding* insofar as the movement toward catastrophe or comic resolution is concerned, *Love's Cruelty* represents an advance upon
the earlier plays in its manipulation of basically dubious tragic ma-
terial. Where the earlier plays fail to reconcile two seemingly in-
compatible modes of dramatic action, *Love's Cruelty* succeeds,
producing a verbal structure unique in Shirley's canon for its deliberate ambiguities, absent from his other plays early and late.

The dominant tragicomic mode in the latter part of his career
occasionally tightened into tragedy or relaxed into city comedy. If
Shirley's style can be said to change at all (no change in sensibility
from *Love Tricks* to *The Constant Maid* or from *The Maid's Revenge*
to *The Cardinal* is discernible), it is in the increasing reliance on
theatrical contrivance. To call a play like *The Lady of Pleasure* a
comedy of manners and to distinguish it in this way from a romantic
comedy such as *The Opportunity* is to overlook the romantic elements in *The Lady of Pleasure* and the concern with manners in
The Opportunity. Both plays are comedies, distinguishable by the
extent to which they depend on disguise, mistaken identity, and
impersonation. Shock tactics in the later tragedies and tragicomedies
take precedence over the inventive plot complications of at least
three of the earlier plays, *Hyde Park, Love's Cruelty*, and *The Lady
of Pleasure*. The last plays of James Shirley are among his least
distinguished.

Nine years after the theaters closed, an Oxford don could allude
to plays as "old" as *Changes* (1632), *The Lady of Pleasure* (1635),
and *The Cardinal* (1641) and expect his readers to be familiar with
them.[6] Whatever he thought of these plays and those by other
dramatists or of the stage generally, the inclusion of references to

Shirley's plays among those to the best-known dramatists of the time (the others: Jonson, Beaumont and Fletcher, Heywood, Randolph, and Ford) confirms the impression of a continuing recognition of Shirley's work for a while after he stopped writing for the stage. During the first decade of the Restoration period, when new plays were at a premium, some of Shirley's work found favor with a variety of London theatergoers, although his plays were not always staged or printed as they were originally written. "Titles were altered and readers were supplied no hint of the existence of original versions."[7] "James Shirley's plays seemed 'safe' " to adapt and produce as if they were new plays by Restoration playwrights. Because they "were so well known," only Shakespeare and Fletcher among native English authors escaped "wholesale appropriation."[8] What this Restoration practice tells us is that the leading London playwright of the Caroline period had apparently lost his reputation within a generation.

References to Shirley or to his work by two well-known Restoration figures are rarely flattering. Samuel Pepys called *Love in a Maze (Changes)* "a sorry play,"[9] but was "mightily pleased" with a production of *The Cardinal* (at the King's Playhouse, Thomas Killigrew's new theater in Lincoln's Inn Fields, which opened November 8, 1660).[10] *"August 18, 1664*. My wife going to-day to see a new play, 'The Court Secret.' . . . My wife says the play she saw is the worst that ever she saw in her life."[11] Pepys himself "sat out" a performance (1667) of *Love's Cruelty* with an actress friend.[12] The production of *Hyde Park* with real horses on stage at the King's theater impressed him.[13] Dryden refers twice to Shirley in *Mac-Flecknoe* (1682): "Heywood and Shirley were but types of thee [Thomas Shadwell], / Thou last great prophet of tautology." "From dusty shops neglected authors come, / Martyrs of pies, and relics of the bum. / Much Heywood, Shirley, Ogleby there lay, / But loads of Sh[adwell] almost chok'd the way."

During the eighteenth century there were few productions of Shirley's plays, and there have been fewer since. Lamb pays attention to him in the *Specimens*, and Swinburne thought *The Example* was his best play.[14] The most influential of twentieth-century critics of seventeenth-century drama, T. S. Eliot, refers to Shirley only in passing, always in company with other dramatists: "Ford and Shirley and Fletcher" as examples of decadence in the drama; "Massinger, or Shirley, or Ford" as metrists; "Beaumont and Fletcher and Shirley as tragedians" among those "whose merit consists merely in having exploited successfully a few Shakespearean devices or echoed here and there the Shakespearean verse"; "Beaumont, Fletcher, Shirley, and Otway," whose "absence of purpose . . . makes their drama tend toward mere sensationalism."[15]

More recently M. C. Bradbrook shows "how entirely the narratives of Shirley's plays depend upon a series of reversals." The "method" is that of "Shirley's predecessors, of Tourneur and Middleton." But "Tourneur's means are Shirley's ends." *The Revenger's Tragedy* and *The Traitor* compared, Bradbrook concludes that Tourneur "can erect an ethic upon his feelings, while Shirley's morality has no general structure. . . ." Yet his "manipulation of the narrative is more ingenious" than Tourneur's. What is left from Shirley's adaptations of *The Revenger's Tragedy* in *The Traitor* and of *The Duchess of Malfi* in *The Cardinal* is empty technique. With reference to *The Maid's Revenge, Love's Cruelty, The Cardinal*, and *The Traitor* Bradbrook finds that "Shirley's tragedies are completely derivative."[16]

Critical opinion of Shirley as belonging to a period of general decline in English Renaissance drama usually emphasizes the lack of inspired poetry. Thus, according to Bradbrook, Shirley is faithful to the Revenge convention except for "that living core which was its justification, the imagery, the peculiar tone, the poetry."[17] Eliot's theory of the mid-seventeenth-century dissociation of sensibility would appear to be applicable to Shirley. The great poets of Shirley's time did not write for the stage, but Eliot saw them as "successors of the dramatists of the sixteenth"[18] in a way that Shirley as dramatist was not. Curiously, *concetti* lifted out of context from Shirley's plays do recall some of Donne's:

> Do'st thinke ther's faith in any womans eyes,
> She wept at parting, a strong obligation
> When they can thread their teares, and make a chaine
> Of water, let me weare one o' their bracelets.
>   (*The Duke's Mistress*, II.i)

>   We will
> Converse in soul, and shoot like Stars, whose Beames
> Are twisted, and make bright the sullen Groves
> Of Lovers as we pass. (*The Doubtful Heir*, II.iii)

Yet in context these conceits distract attention from the action instead of enhancing it, for they attenuate dramatic utterance by substituting wit for conflict where they should be combining the two. The mental energy of Shirley's wit cannot conceal an emotional torpidity, and, paradoxically, reveals an intellectual stasis where conflicting emotions in Donne's speakers stimulate active thought and vice versa. Surprisingly, Shirley seems to be aware of the concept of "dissociation of sensibility" when he has Honorio in *The Imposture* (in soliloquy, incidentally) yearn for a psychic rebirth:

> Virtue and honor, I allow you names,
> You,may give matter for dispute, and noise,
> But you have lost your Essence, and that truth
> We fondly have believ'd in human soules,
> Is ceas'd to be, we are grown fantastick bodies,
> Figures, and empty titles, and make hast
> To our first nothing, he that will be honest,
> Must quite throw off his cold decrepit nature,
> And have a new creation. (V.ii)

Awareness of a split between thinking and feeling seems only to have intensified Shirley's distrust of strong emotion and not to have led him to explore it beyond its conformity (or lack of it) to a rigid code of noble behavior. The self-sacrificing heroes and heroines of his tragedies and tragicomedies may suffer emotional storms (his favorite image for inner conflicts) that match the villainous characters' equally passionate outbursts, but the expression of turbulence usually only describes it, without suggesting any doubt about the value of the standard against which excessive emotion is measured. Whatever eloquence Shirley's dramatic verse boasts belongs to an order of sensibility not congenial to great drama. Shirley is at his best when he is tracing the course of simple emotions, as in Albina's speech in the last act of *The Politician*, where the language is plain, the comparisons few, and the sentences short. The variations in the blank-verse line are many: there is a good deal of enjambment, the broken rhythms heightening the sense of precariously controlled emotion in the passage beginning "If pittie dwell within your royal bosom" and ending "can you or any tell me / Where I may find the comfort of mine eies, / My husband; or but tell me that he lives, / And I will pray for you—then he is dead / Indeed I feare" (V.ii). The basic regularity of the measure makes the speech a formal rendering of Albina's feelings. The references to past personal griefs, the ambivalence of Albina's feelings about her dead husband, and the questions addressed to any who will listen combine to create a rhetorically effective expression of grief over the loss of a loved one. Shirley's taste for formality works here to display a gift for portraying pathos.

Most scholars and critics today acknowledge Shirley's achievements in comedy without insisting on its anticipating the Restoration dramatists', for "the plays of Etherege, Wycherley, and Congreve simply do not fit comfortably into the comedy-romance tradition of Lyly, Shakespeare, and Shirley into which they have often been forced"[19]—and thus often obscuring the intrinsic merits of Shirley's best comedies. Shirley indeed writes best when he is evoking the spirit of morally enlightened urbanity, as in *The Lady of Pleasure* and *Hyde Park*. The constricting conservatism, simplistic psychology, and solemn moralizing that weaken his tragedies and tragicomedies provide strong ballast for the best of his comedies. In *The Lady of Pleasure* and *Hyde Park* Shirley makes a lasting contribution to English drama. Enough attention is paid to sex and money to keep the two plays from becoming fantastic compliments to the London gentry. *The Lady of Pleasure* and *Hyde Park* have substance as well as style and wit; they present an attractive image of a world where honor and *politesse* thrive.

Shirley, with Inigo Jones, created the most splendid masque of the Caroline period. An art form so closely associated with royalty could hardly survive the Interregnum (although *Cupid and Death* was staged for the Portuguese ambassador). Italian opera, already known to the English in the late Elizabethan and Stuart eras, may have superseded the masque by the time of the Restoration. Or perhaps English operas such as *Dido and Aeneas* rendered it passé. In any case Shirley mastered the form at the height of its relatively brief vogue.

The playwright who began his career with such promise and high hopes in 1625 worked for ten years in congenial company and for seven more under increasingly difficult conditions. Shirley wrote regularly and steadily in good times and bad, producing three fine plays during the earlier period, *Love's Cruelty*, *The Lady of Pleasure*, and *Hyde Park*, and several worthwhile ones in both periods, including *Love Tricks*, *The Witty Fair One*, *The Example*, *The Gentleman of Venice*, and *The Cardinal*, that, for all their shortcomings, rank well above the average theater fare of the Caroline period. If even at his best Shirley suffers by comparison with the giants and near-giants of English Renaissance drama, it is because talent, not genius, marks the work of their industrious successor.

Notes and References

Chapter One

1. *Athenae Oxonienses* (1692), ed. Philip Bliss, 4 v. (Hildesheim, Germany: Georg Olms Verlagsbuchhandlung, 1969), v. 3, 737. Hereafter cited as Wood.

2. John Gould Nichols, ed., *History from Marble* (Camden Society, 1867; repr. Johnson Reprint Corporation, 1968), Series No. 1, v. 94, xiii. Most descriptions of this coat of arms refer to *"quarter* ermine" (italics added). "Canton" seems fit for a Cantabrigian. Nichols quotes directly from *Alphabett of Arms* by Dingley, a student of Shirley's in the 1650s.

3. Shirley maintained at least some connection with one prominent Shirley family during his London career, for he dedicated *Changes, or Love in a Maze* in 1632 to "the Right Honourable the Lady Dorothy Shirley."

4. *James Shirley, Dramatist* (1915; repr. New York: Benjamin Blom, Inc., 1967), pp. 8-20.

5. Wood, p. 737.

6. According to two documents of 1624 Shirley was not yet a Catholic: see Georges Bas, "Two Misrepresented Biographical Documents Concerning James Shirley," *RES* 27 (NS 1976): 303-10. The alleged misrepresentation is Albert C. Baugh's in "Some New Facts about Shirley," *MLR* 17 (1922): 228-35. See also Bas's "James Shirley, Pasteur dans le Hertfordshire," *EA* 15 (1962): 266-68. On September 19, 1619, according to a document in the Bishop of London's Registry, "Jacobus Sherley B.A., of Catherine Hall, Cambridge, about 24 years of age, a native of the Parish of St. Mary, Woolchurch (Haw) London, [was] ordained Deacon by Bishop John King and instituted to the Curacy of Wheathampstead in the Country of Lincoln [*sic*]."

7. Donald S. Lawless, "A Further Note on Shirley's Religion," *N&Q* 24 (NS 1977): 543.

8. In "Annals of the Careers of James and Henry Shirley," *Anglia* 8 (1885): 405-14, F. G. Fleay's entry for 1623 referring to James Shirley states unequivocally that Shirley "adopted the Roman Catholic belief." Izaak Walton admits "in his will, dated 9 August 1683, to 'a very long and very true friendship with some of the *Roman* church' "—presumably including Shirley. But, Bas points out, Walton refers nowhere in his extant writings to Shirley, except for misquoting or adapting the last four lines of "The Glories." ("Thomas Zouch's Life of Walton and the Alleged Friendship Between James Shirley and Izaak Walton," *N&Q* 24 [NS 1977]: 125-26.) In addition Bas quotes a footnote from Zouch's Life of Walton, which accompanied an edition of Walton's *Lives* published in 1796: "A steady

146

friendship subsisted between Walton and James Shirley, the dramatist, who, having been ordained a Clergyman of the established Church, renounced his religion for that of the Church of Rome" (p. 125). It is on the basis of such dubious "evidence" as this, which Bas thinks Zouch probably got from Wood's *Athenae Oxonienses,* that Shirley is reputed to have converted to Catholicism. Donald S. Lawless, in "A Further Note on Shirley's Religion," *N&Q,* 24 [NS 1977]: 543, writes: "In commendatory verses prefixed to Shirley's *Via ad Latinam Linguam Complanata* (1649), his friend Brome wrote in part:

> And to thy memory, fame shall this enroul,
> Who ere the Church, thou dost reform the School.

Obviously, Brome is calling attention to Shirley's church—a matter . . . unnecessary if Shirley belonged to the Established Church." But is Richard Brome indeed "singling out Shirley's church for some reason or other"? Or is he calling attention to the universal value of Shirley's teaching to members of every Christian denomination? As for internal evidence, consider the Reverend Stephen J. Radtke's *James Shirley: His Catholic Philosophy of Life* (Washington, D.C.: The Catholic University of America, 1929), p. 65: "A remarkable feature of the play is the rather frequent reference to prayer and its efficacy, especially prayers for the dead, showing the author's characteristic of inculcating Catholic religious principles." Radtke is referring to *The Doubtful Heir*. He notes frequent references in *The Grateful Servant* to the Benedictines and "a situation" in *The Gentleman of Venice's* last act, "which Shirley has handled in true Catholic fashion." Cornari, disguised as a Black Friar, "does not attempt to abuse the sacred tribunal of the confessional" (p. 68). Gerald Eades Bentley, in *The Jacobean and Caroline Stage* (Oxford: Clarendon Press, 1941-68), notes (v. 2, 573) that Shirley's "Catholicism has been generally assumed," but that "some documentary evidence of it would be welcome." And still unexplained is the Puritan government's leniency after the Civil War: as a supporter of the late king, Shirley was fined only lightly by the new regime, which imposed harsher penalties on known and suspected Catholics.

9. Shirley may have written a number of poems commemorating Stanley's marriage to Dorothea Enyon. See G. E. Bentley, "James Shirley and a Group of Unnoted Poems on the Wedding of Thomas Stanley," *MLQ* 2 (1939): 219-32. Bentley offers evidence from prefaces, dedications, commendatory verses, and commemorative poems that "Shirley for a time . . . beginning probably in 1644 or 1645, was a member of a group about Thomas Stanley and was probably in his patronage." The other members of the Stanley group were his uncle, William Hammond, and three young scholars (Edward Sherburne, William Fairfax, John Hall).

10. "The smoke of one's native land is brighter than the fire of a foreign country."

11. Nichols, v. 94, 25.

12. *Via ad Latinam Linguam Complanata* (The Way Made Plain to the Latin Tongue), 1649; *The Rudiments of Grammar*, 1656; *Manductio: or, A Leading of Children by the Hand Through the Principles of Grammar*, 1660.

13. Joseph Frank, ed., *Hobbled Pegasus* (Albuquerque: University of New Mexico Press, 1968), p. 367.

14. (Menston, England: Scolar Press, 1971.) This is a facsimile of the first edition published in London by Joseph Downing, 1726.

15. Most historians find that the king's support came from a minority, mainly in the House of Lords, not from the gentry or the working class. The 1630s began with domestic crop failures and an economic depression in trade, which could have been mitigated by enforcement of laws regarding relief for the indigent. But Charles's so-called "Personal Rule" tolerated a corrupt administration. Before the civil war actually started, Archbishop Laud and the Earl of Strafford, the most powerful proponents of Charles's cause, were imprisoned, the Long Parliament abolished the Star Chamber, a rebellion broke out in Ireland (1641), and the Royal Family left London. By midsummer of 1642 Englishmen began fighting Englishmen over control of the militia, and thus a seven-year civil war began. By the mid-1640s the more widely supported Cromwell was reaching a political position of the greatest prominence; by 1649 the war was over, and Charles was executed for treason.

16. John Donne, *"The First Sermon Preached to King Charles, at Saint James:* 3°. April. 1625. Text: Psalme II.3. If the Foundations Be Destroyed, What Can the Righteous Do?" Sermon Number 12 in vol. 6 of *The Sermons of John Donne*, 10 vols., eds. Evelyn M. Simpson and George R. Potter (Berkeley and Los Angeles: University of California Press, 1953), p. 245.

17. Donne, p. 254. Donne's purpose in this sermon may well have been to caution the new King about the danger of Catholicism, for, like many English Protestants, Donne was concerned about Henrietta Maria's influence on Charles. But more relevant to the present discussion is the notion of a king's sacred mission, a notion not confined to Catholics.

18. Shirley uses these terms of hierarchy most frequently: *emperor, prince, queen, sovereign, kingdom, sceptre, crown, regency, throne; cavalier, courtier, gentleman, lordship, knighthood, champion, general, officer; common persons, villains, cowards, slaves*. The *top boughs* are the *protectors* of the *state*. One's *name, title, birth, condition* (status), or *degree* determines his *place* in the *commonwealth*. The *blood* in the *veins* of *governors*, their *family*, their *breeding*, their *highness* and *greatness* qualify them for their *offices* of *power* and for *additions of state*. *Subject* and *vassal* acknowledge the *difference* between their *fortune* and that of those who *rule* by *begging, kneeling, saluting, pleading*. They are *humble* ("humbly beg your grace"). The *valiant* military *command* seeks *glory* in *war* with *sword* and *daring*. *Conquest* brings a *glorious wreath, garlands, laurel,*

largess, bounty, compensation, wealth, maintenance, pension from the *treasury* or *exchequer*.

The key terms of order in a princely state include *duty, allegiance, obedience, promise, oath, royal word, ceremony, courtesy, loyalty, constancy, security, service,* and *faithfulness*. The ideal subject helps to maintain order by his *devotion* to *duty* and by *patience* in awaiting a *prince's pleasure* or *gratitude*, with a possible *reward*. The key terms of disorder are *tyrant, imperiousness, unprincely entertainment; mutinous thoughts, conspiracy, betrayal, opposition, insurrection, traitor, treason, rebel, usurper, impostor, counterfeit, apostasy; dissension, discontents, impiety, audacity, insolence, boldness, threat, affront, injury, saucy, impudent, disgrace, blemish, stain,* and *revenge*. The subject guilty of a *breach of duty* must pay a *penalty*, often *banishment* or *exile*, for his *offence*. Revolt against tyrannical princes in the tragedies and tragicomedies may be as justifiable as virtuous lovers' rebellion against tyrannical parents in the comedies, but Shirley never suggests that authority figures should not have unlimited power, only that they should use it wisely.

The *sacred title* and the *sacred person* of *king* or *emperor* should inspire *awe* and *trembling*. A prince is due *reverence* as well as *esteem*. A subject performs his *sacred duty* to a king out of loyalty to a system of government blessed by God. *Obsequiousness* to a prince or *sovereign* implies nothing *base* or *common*. On the contrary it bespeaks *duty* and *devotion*. By his *sufferance, grace,* or *charity* a prince may *descend* or *stoop* or *deign* to share intimacies with his inferiors, as Rosaura does with her ladies-in-waiting in *The Cardinal*. The threat to the institution of monarchy comes not from a dissident group, for even civil war means only a change of monarchs, but from a self-seeker at court. In the tragicomedies a prince may grant *pardon* or show *mercy* to the *rebel*, the *traitor*, and the *favorite* who has committed sacrilege by betraying his trust. (The Duke in *The Royal Master*, a tragicomedy, lightens his erstwhile favorite Montalto's punishment from death to banishment.)

The schemer can be recognized by his eloquence: "Y'are too bountifull / In language sir" (*The Imposture*, I.ii), observes Leonato, the conquering hero, after a long welcoming encomium, which Gifford describes as "studiously inflated and bombastic," marking "the insincerity of the speaker." (William Gifford and Alexander Dyce, eds., *The Dramatic Works and Poems of James Shirley*, V [1833; rpt. New York: Russell and Russell, 1966], 190 n.) Leonato himself is sincere in his admiration of the former imposter Juliana, who responds to his praises with "My lord, our study here [a convent] is life, not language" (II.iii). (Juliet McGrath deals at some length with Shirley's own distrust of language in "James Shirley's Uses of Language," *Studies in English Literature 1500–1900* 6 [1966]: 323–39.) False or sincere, then, studied language is suspect, an unreliable imitation of life. The solid citizen Goldsworth in *Changes, or Love in a Maze* urges poets not to "lard" (embellish) language. For those matters whose truth is un-assailable, such as the divinity of kingship, no embellishment is necessary.

The character to whom the following lines are addressed happens to feel powerless, but the sentiment expressed applies to princes generally: "Your power on earth's divine, Princes are here / The Coppies of eternity, and create / When they but will our happiness" (*The Coronation*, I.i). "Subjects may love as their rude sense imparts, / But heaven doth onely govern Princes hearts" (*The Opportunity*, V.ii. closing couplet). A prince carries a burden of responsibility the private man is spared: "*Private men meet the force of common stings, / But none can feel the weight of Kings but Kings*" (*The Court Secret*, IV.iii). Even a prince of rogues, the bandit Frapolo in *The Sisters*, can express in a comic context the truth of the sacred bond between ruler and ruled: " 'Tis time your Prince were dead," announces Frapolo as he faces an uprising, "and when I am / Companion to my Fathers dust, these tumults / Fomented by seditious men, that are / Weary of Plenty, and delights of Peace, / Shall not approach to interrupt the calm / Good Princes after Death enjoy." As ruler, Frapolo has brought prosperity to his "subjects" and maintained peace: that is how a ruler serves the ruled: "Go home, / I pray depart, I rather will submit / To be depos'd, than wear a power or title / That shall not all be dedicate to serve you." And a good ruler is ready to sacrifice himself, for "My life is but the gift of Heaven, to wast it / For your dear sakes." The ruler is like a father: "My people are my Children, / Whom I am bound in Nature and Religion / To Cherish and protect." The ruler is impartial in the administration of justice, without regard for status: "Perhaps you have / Some grievance to present, you shall have justice / Against the proudest here; I look not on / Nobility of Birth, Office, or Fortunes, / The poorest subject has a Native Charter, / And a Birth-right to th'Laws, and Commonwealth, / Which, with an equall, and impartial stream, / Shall flow to every bosom." This speech of Frapolo's from *The Sisters* (V.ii), one of the last plays Shirley wrote before civil war broke out, epitomizes the reverence Shirley felt for royalty.

19. James Howell, letter dated June 3, 1634, in Joseph Jacobs, ed., *The Familiar Letters of James Howell* (London, 1890), pp. 317–18, as quoted by Richard C. Harrier, ed., *Jacobean Drama*, II (New York: Doubleday, 1963; rpt. The Norton Library, 1968), xviii.

20. *The Tragic Muse of John Ford* (Stanford: Stanford University Press, 1944), p. 108. For a refutation of Sensabaugh's interpretation of coterie plays, see Ronald Huebert, *John Ford, Baroque English Dramatist* (Montreal and London: McGill-Queen's University Press, 1977), pp. 198–99.

21. Sensabaugh, pp. 109–32.

22. John Bruce, ed., *Charles I. in 1646: Letters of King Charles the First to Queen Henrietta Maria* (London: Camden Society, 1856), passim.

23. Quentin Bone, *Henrietta Maria: Queen of the Cavaliers* (Urbana: University of Illinois Press, 1972), p. 85. Henrietta Maria gave birth to eight children between 1630 and 1644. Her participation in "cult" activities

was probably limited to a few appearances in court theatricals. Bone does not even mention a "love cult" in his biography, "a study of Henrietta's significance in English politics" (p. v).

24. The lost plays are probably *The Tragedy of St. Albans* and *Look to the Ladie,* written and produced in Dublin during Shirley's stay there (1636–40), but never printed. Plays of doubtful authorship include *Love Will Find out the Way* and *The Arcadia.* T. J. King identifies *Love* (1661) as a revision of *The Constant Maid,* with T. B. (Theophilus Bird?) listed as author on the titlepage. T. B. may have revised the play for a Restoration production, for it includes more lines and songs than the first edition of 1640. See T. J. King, "Shirley's *Coronation* and *Love Will Find out the Way:* Erroneous Title-Pages," *SB* 18 (1965): 265–69. *The Arcadia* is the only play of its kind in the Shirley canon, if it belongs there. If indeed he wrote it some time between 1627 and 1630 (as Robert S. Forsythe suggests in *The Relations of Shirley's Plays to the Elizabethan Drama,* p. 271), years during which no plays by Shirley were licensed, it represents a departure from the kind of plays (city comedies, tragedies) with which he began his writing for the theater. The dramatization of Sidney's pastoral romance follows the narrative line of the original with some minor omissions, but no interpolations. Some passages, such as the record of the oracle that led King Basilius to leave his court for the country, are lifted intact from Sidney. There are several very funny passages in *The Arcadia,* as there are in the original.

Shirley included among his professional tasks revisions of other dramatists' work, especially when he was in Dublin, where he also wrote prologues and epilogues for their plays. Whether he ever collaborated with another playwright is doubtful, although "joint authorship was a commonplace in the repertory of the King's company, at least from 1616 to 1642." See Gerald Eades Bentley, *The Profession of Dramatist in Shakespeare's Time 1590–1642* (Princeton: Princeton University Press, 1971), p. 20. Plays revised by Shirley include *The Careless Shepherdess,* by Thomas Goffe; *The Night Walker,* by John Fletcher; and *Chabot,* by George Chapman. *The Careless Shepherdess* includes a song from Shirley's *The Triumph of Beauty* and several allusions to events that occurred after Goffe's death. (See Bentley, *The Jacobean and Caroline Stage,* v. 4, 501–505.) Shirley may have assisted in the writing and indeed may have been the "principal author" of two plays, *The Country Captain* and *The Variety,* attributed to William Cavendish, Duke of Newcastle. (See Bentley, *The Profession of Dramatist,* p. 20.)

The extent of Shirley's revisions of *The Night Walker* and *Chabot* has engaged the attention of several scholars, including Cyrus Hoy, who makes frequent mention of Shirley in his series of *Studies in Bibliography* articles (1956–59), "The Shares of Fletcher and his Collaborators in the Beaumont and Fletcher Canon." Hoy says that "modern scholarship is agreed that less than twelve" of the plays attributed to Beaumont and Fletcher "are indeed products of their joint authorship" (*SB* 8 [1956]: 129). Among the many playwrights "suggested as candidates" for collaboration with one or the other—or with Philip Massinger, for that matter ("whose share in the plays of the corpus can be demonstrated beyond any doubt")—is Shirley (ibid.). "In the case of such dramatists as Field, Shirley and Ford, it will be seen . . . that linguistic evidence provides a more certain basis for assigning their share in the plays of the [Beaumont and Fletcher] canon than has yet been available" (*SB* 8 [1956]: 130). *"The Night Walker,* originally one of Fletcher's unaided plays," was "revised in its extant text by Shirley" (*SB* 8 [1956]: 134). "Fletcher's comedy of *The Night Walker* was, as we know from the Office-Book of Sir Henry Herbert, revised by Shirley in the 1630's; this external evidence for Shirley's revision is corroborated . . . by the internal linguistic evidence which the first quarto text of the play affords" (*SB* 12 [1959]: 91).

With reference to *Chabot,* attributed to both Chapman and Shirley, Eugene M. Waith writes: "Some of the dramatic effectiveness is probably due to James Shirley, a man of the theatre *par excellence,* who apparently revised the play about a year before its publication in 1635." See *Ideas of Greatness* (New York: Barnes and Noble, Inc., 1971), pp. 124–41. Allen Bergson includes *Chabot,* without mention of Shirley's possible collaboration or revision, among those of Chapman's latest tragedies, described as "Stoic," differing from Shakespearean tragedy (with its "tragic movement toward integration of self") and from ironic tragedy, such as Chapman's own *Bussy D'Ambois* (with its "ironic-tragic movement toward the fragmentation and loss of self"). See "The Ironic Tragedies of Marston and Chapman: Notes on Jacobean Tragic Form," *JEGP* 69 (1970): 615. Derek Crawley does not consider the play a collaboration, and he distinguishes between the parts that he thinks were written separately by analyzing selected passages for evidence of Stoicism (Chapman) or lack of it (Shirley). In addition, those parts perhaps written by Shirley feature female characters prominently, "stage action such as kneeling and swooning," sentimentality, excessive emotion; those by Chapman, intricate sentence structure, "grandiosity," and a "heavily moral flavor." He concludes that "Shirley's interest in emotional scenes has often undermined Chapman's interest in moral teaching." See "The Effect of Shirley's Hand on Chapman's *The Tragedy of Chabot Admiral of France," SP* 63 (1966): 677–96. A. R. Braunmuller, in " 'A Greater Wound': Corruption and Human Frailty in Chapman's 'Chabot, Admiral of France,' " *MLR* 70 (1975): 241–59, does not claim that Shirley did not revise the play ("however much Shirley may have handled it," p. 242), but he argues that "Shirley found (and perhaps highlighted) elements which were already present in Chapman's original work (p. 243)." Both collaboration and revision remain matters of speculation, but with only a small part of the Shirley canon.

25. *The Profession of Dramatist,* p. 37.
26. Ibid., p. 89.

27. Russell Fraser, *The War Against Poetry* (Princeton: Princeton University Press, 1970), p. 14.

28. In "the 1570s in England . . . stage plays begin to be classified among unregenerate forms of entertainment," ibid., p. 12.

29. "A Prologue to the / ALCHIMIST / Acted (in *Ireland*)," quoted in full in *Ben Jonson*, C. H. Herford, Percy and Evelyn Simpson, eds., 11 vols. (Oxford: Clarendon Press, 1925–52), v. 9, 226.

30. Shirley's preface to the 1647 folio of *The Works of Beaumont and Fletcher*, ed. George Darley (London: Routledge, Warde, and Routledge, 1840), p. xliv.

31. George C. Herndl, *The High Design: English Renaissance Tragedy and the Natural Law* (Lexington: The University Press of Kentucky, 1970), p. 228. However, in the comedies, according to Frieder Stadtfeld, Shirley "nicht nur die 'Charackterbrüche' der Fletcherschen Tragikomödien zu parodieren verstand, sondern . . . er auch den Erwartungen eines hellhörigen und für witzige *equivocations* empfänglichen Publikums entgegenzukommen wusste." " 'Fortune,' 'providence' und 'manners' in James Shirleys *Hyde Park*," *Anglia* 93 (1975): 116.

32. G. R. Hibbard, "Love, Marriage and Money in Shakespeare's Theatre and Shakespeare's England," *The Elizabethan Theatre VI* (Hamden, Conn.: Shoe String Press, 1975), pp. 141–42.

33. Martin J. Havran, *The Catholics in Caroline England* (Stanford: Stanford University Press, 1962), p. 19. As for "plots," C. V. Wedgwood observes that Charles "had always had a taste for intrigue, and his plots were unceasing and often of a self-contradictory complexity." *A Coffin for King Charles (The Trial and Execution of Charles I)* (New York: The Macmillan Co., 1964), p. 10.

34. Bone, p. 18.

35. Shirley's direct indebtedness to Spanish literature can be illustrated by his borrowings from Lope de Vega, Tirso de Molina, and Cervantes. Shirley's indebtedness to classical literature is more general. Senecan tragedy, to which all revenge tragedy was indebted, was certainly "in the public domain," although of the dozen new complete editions of Seneca's tragedies in the original tongue published in Europe 1625–42, only one edition was published in England (1634); no new English translations of Seneca appeared during this time. In any case Shirley the accomplished Latinist would have consulted the original.

36. Robert S. Forsythe has studied Shirley parallel passages exhaustively in *The Relations of Shirley's Plays to the Elizabethan Drama* (New York: Columbia University Press, 1914; rpt. New York: Benjamin Blom, Inc., 1965).

37. Similarly, the London playhouses for which Shirley wrote were not much different, as far as physical properties are concerned, from those of the Elizabethans and Jacobeans. D. F. Rowan argues persuasively, from "evidence, both graphic and textual," that there are no significant structural

differences among the playhouses of the period 1595–1630 (and perhaps 1576–1642), whether "public," "private," or "court." "The English Play-house: 1595–1630," *Renaissance Drama* 4 (1971): 37-51.

38. *A Contention* contains references to Moorfields and Bow-bell; *The Ball*, to Cheapside, Bankside, St. Paul's, the Exchange, Paddington, Fish-street, Hyde Park, Spring Garden, Bear-garden; *The Constant Maid*, to Bedlam, Islington (and such diverse matters as Shrove Tuesday, May-Day, Perkin Warbeck, the Star Chamber, Dick Whittington, and Michael Angelo, as he was known to Englishmen at the time); *The Gamester*, to the Strand and Westminster; *Honoria and Mammon*, to Bridewell.

39. See also *Honoria and Mammon* ("rich Peru," "My America," and "My Indies"); *The Court Secret* ("Indies"—and Columbus); *The Example* ("Bermudas"); and *A Contention* (to come from America is to be an "infidel born").

Chapter Two

1. Stephen Orgel writes that "the masque was for Jonson a form of idealizing poetry. The sorts of contexts and personae he provided for his masquers were realizations of those he created for the heroes of his society in works like the epistle to Sir Robert Wroth, *To Penshurst*, and the various addresses to the Countess of Bedford." "The Poetics of Spectacle," *New Literary History* 2 (1971): 386.

2. John G. Demaray observes that Jonson "was replaced by four sub-missive writers—Aurelian Townshend, James Shirley, Thomas Carew, and William Davenant—all of whom were generally willing to subordinate po-etry to stage spectacle in the nine court masques they wrote in turn before the overthrow of the English monarchy in the 1640's." These masques "reflect the aims of Inigo Jones. The designer, in stressing stage spectacle, sacrificed both the allegorical 'hinge' and the structure, and produced long, lavish, episodic shows." Perhaps Shirley cannot be held responsible for the clutter of *The Triumph of Peace*. Demaray notes, too: "Later, when Shirley was free of the influence of both the King and Inigo Jones, he wrote two masques, *The Triumph of Beauty* (1646) and *Cupid and Death* (1653), each containing only one antimasque and generally following the Jonsonian struc-tural pattern. . . . *The Triumph of Peace* . . . was a series of spectacles rather than an integrated work of art." *Milton and the Masque Tradition* (Cambridge, Mass.: Harvard University Press, 1968), pp. 59–60, 69–70.

3. Demaray, p. 69.

4. W. W. Greg, "*The Triumph of Peace*: A Bibliographer's Nightmare," *Library* 5th Series, 1 (1946–47): 114.

5. Eugene M. Waith describes Jonson's masques, particularly, as "cel-ebrations of political order and of the qualities of mind and temperament traditionally associated with the maintenance of this order—valor, love of justice, and magnanimity. In other words, the politics of the masque are

heroic, the platform, encomium of the man who can bring into being an ideal society. That this man should be monarch is no departure from heroic precedent. . . ." "Spectacles of State," *Studies in English Literature, 1500–1900* 13 (1973): 326.

6. The second production was a private entertainment, apparently officially sanctioned; the third, again official and "public." The music by Locke and Gibbons may have been composed only for the two performances in 1659. See R. G. Howarth, "Shirley's *Cupid and Death,*" *Times Literary Supplement,* 15 November 1934, p. 795.

7. Bentley, *The Jacobean and Caroline Stage,* v. 5, 1119.

8. Three pairs of legitimate lovers and a fourth made up of a fool and a transvestite appear in the masque that the poetaster Caperwit devises and presents at the end of *Changes.*

9. *The Poems of James Shirley* (Morningside Heights, N.Y.: King's Crown Press, 1941). Armstrong's edition collates all earlier editions of Shirley's verse, except for R. G. Howarth's "The Poems of James Shirley," which "exists only as a typewritten copy guarded by the triple brass of the English School Library at Oxford." Armstrong, introduction, p. xiii.

10. Armstrong, p. xvii.

Chapter Three

1. *The Arcadia* (see Chapter 1, n. 24) and *The Tragedy of St. Albans* also belong to this period. Shirley refers to *The Maid's Tragedy* as his "second birth in this kind" (tragedy): "The first was probably the lost *Tragedy of St. Albans.*" Bentley, *The Jacobean and Caroline Stage,* v. 5, 1133.

2. The question is examined by Nason, pp. 47–69. Nason opts for 1641 as the date of composition and for *The Politique Father* as the original title of the play published in 1652 as *The Brothers.* He points out that the dedication to Thomas Stanley could not reasonably have been written in 1626, when Stanley was only one year old. But of course the dedication need not have been written at the same time as the play.

3. W. W. Skeat and A. L. Mayhew, *A Glossary of Tudor and Stuart Words* (Oxford, 1914; rpt. New York: Burt Franklin, 1968).

4. "Shirley's *The Wedding* and the Marriage of Sir Kenelm Digby," *Philological Quarterly* 16 (1937): 35.

Chapter Four

1. The source of the play has engaged some attention since Forsythe discovered a number of historical parallels to incidents in it. A. P. Riemer says that the Pisano-Oriana sub-plot is "based closely on an account" of a thirteenth-century murder "which Shirley found in Thomas Bedingfield's translation of Macchiavelli's *Le Istorie Fiorentine*" (*The Florentine Historie of Nicholo Machiavelli,* published in London in 1595, pp. 29–30), "A Source

for Shirley's *The Traitor,*" *RES* 14 (1963): 380. "Bedingfield's version is
. . . the only account of the story in English which was available to Shirley
to use, and there is little doubt that he obtained it from there" (p. 381).
John Stewart Carter, ed., *The Traitor* (Lincoln: University of Nebraska,
1965), p. v, notes that "whether Shirley used an Italian history, or one
published in England and now lost sight of, must remain a matter of con-
jecture for the present."

2. *The Humourous Courtier* has been identified as *The Duke*, a play
by Shirley produced in 1631, but never published. No record of production
of *The Humourous Courtier* appears in Edmund Malone's transcription of
Sir Henry Herbert's lists of plays licensed for production from 1623 to 1642.
The first edition of *The Humourous Courtier*, in quarto, appeared in 1640.
See Marvin Morillo, ed., James Shirley's *The Humourous Courtier* (New
York and London: Garland Publishing, Inc., 1979), pp. 1–96.

3. *The Ball* has been attributed to George Chapman as well as to Shirley.
It "is the joint production of Chapman and Shirley" (Gifford, *Works*, v. 3,
3). Both are listed on the title-page of the 1639 edition. Hanson T. Parlin
argues persuasively that "Shirley is . . . the sole author" (*A Study in Shirley's Comedies of London Life*, Bulletin of the University of Texas, No. 371
[Nov. 15, 1914], iii). "Chapman really had nothing to do with *The Ball*"
(Bentley, *The Jacobean and Caroline Stage*, v. 5, 1078).

4. Commentary on *Hyde Park* has been most enlightening, however,
in pointing out parallels with the proviso scene in Restoration comedies.
Typically it is "a scene of wit combat between two lovers in which they
establish conditions for marriage," and in which the woman generally makes
all the conditions, while the man makes none. Yvonne Bonsall Shafer, "The
Proviso Scene in Restoration Comedy," *RECTR* 9 (1970): 1. *Hyde Park* is
cited as an example of such a scene in earlier English drama.

5. The Hyde Park scenes in Acts III and IV are "an integral part of the
comedy and vital to both its structure and meaning." Albert Wertheim,
"Games and Courtship in James Shirley's *Hyde Park*," *Anglia* 90 (1972):
71.

6. The multiple-plot structure has had various other interpretations,
not mutually exclusive. "All the plots of *Hyde Park*, as well as the symbolic
horse and foot races, depend on the defeat of a confident, seemingly favored,
competitor" (Wertheim, p. 75). *Hyde Park* has an "internal coherence in
its over-all comic structure" to which "the special environment of the Park
is subordinated" (Richard Levin, "The Triple Plot of *Hyde Park*," *MLR* 62
[1967]: 17). Levin compares the tripartite comic-plot structure of *Hyde Park*
to that of *The Ball, The Gamester,* and *The Lady of Pleasure*. In *Hyde Park*
the main plot is "a sophisticated or 'high' comedy of clever intrigue . . .;
the second is a sentimental comedy . . .; and the third a simple comedy
of situation that depends mainly . . . upon coincidence, disguise, and sheer
spectacle" (p. 25).

7. *Hyde Park* was "the first racing play on record. Shirley's fourth act presented most of the excitements of a foot race and a horse race in a realistic way, even to the confused noise of the gamblers; but there was one noteworthy omission. For, whereas in the foot race the competitors crossed the stage twice, not a glimpse of the thoroughbreds was vouchsafed throughout. The horse race was conveyed imaginatively by illusive sounds and shouts without. Perhaps one could not better illustrate the essential difference between platform-stage principles and picture-stage principles than by the fact that when *Hyde Park* came to be revived at the Theatre Royal in 1668 it was deemed requisite to bring in real horses. Now that the public had become habituated to the use of scenery, the imagination could no longer be trusted to do its work." William J. Lawrence, *Pre-Restoration Stage Studies* (Cambridge, Mass.: Harvard University Press, 1927; rpt. New York: Benjamin Blom, 1967), pp. 275-76.

8. John Quincy Adams, ed., *The Dramatic Records of Sir Henry Herbert, Master of the Revels 1623–1673* (1917; rpt. New York: Benjamin Blom, Inc., 1963), p. 19.

9. Among the many military figures treated sympathetically in Shirley's plays, Winfield represents the best of his profession. See *The Young Admiral,* I.ii, III.i, and III.ii; *The Example,* III.i; *The Gentleman of Venice,* IV.ii; *The Politician,* III.i, V.ii; *Honoria and Mammon,* I.ii, II.iii (substantially the same speech appears in *A Contention for Honour and Riches,* an early version of *Honoria and Mammon); The Opportunity,* I.ii; the scenes involving Volterino and Hortensio, army colonels, in *The Imposture;* and those involving the Captain in *The Doubtful Heir.* Shirley's military men reflect, as do all his characters, prevailing Royalist views of society and the individual. Shirley measures the value of individualism by the degree to which it allows members of any class to meet its function; that is, he places little value on truth to one's own nature if it is in conflict with the social truth of class distinction. Each class has an ideal representative, such as Winfield in *The Ball,* on whom members of that class should model themselves.

10. Cosmo's sophistries are worthy of the cynical speakers of some of Donne's songs and sonnets:

> Let us examine all the creatures, reade
> The booke of Nature through, and we shall finde
> Nothing doth still the same, the stars do wander,
> And have their divers influence, the Elements
> Shuffle into innumerable changes:
> Our constitutions varie, Hearbs, and Trees
> Admit their Frosts and Summer: and why then
> Should our desires, that are so nimble, and
> More subtill then the spirits in our blood,
> Be such stayd things within us, and not share
> Their naturall liberty, shall we admit a change

> In smaller of things, and not allow it in
> What most of all concernes us? (II.ii)

Chapter Five

1. The characterization of Peregrine is in itself an "example" Shirley is using to gain sympathy for the soldier class. Military men have financial problems because they are underpaid. Peregrine joined the army because he was poor, but after a long period in the service, he still cannot pay his debts: "I have made / No purchase but of wounds, since my departure. / I have paide some debts of warre, but cannot promise / To cancell one, that threatens mee at home" (III.i).

2. Such an interpretation of Confident Rapture's role in *The Example* would be reinforced by Nathan Cogan's analysis of the play's structure in "James Shirley's *The Example* (1634): Some Reconsiderations," *SEL* 17 (1977): 317–31. "The contrast between idealized and libertine attitudes toward love remains its most potent principle of form" (p. 331). "*The Example* represents and analyzes a London social morality far more penetrating in its skeptical slant and moral ambiguity than Swinburne, or even Arthur Nason, would have been willing to perceive" (ibid.).

3. Swinburne, who calls *The Example* "the best of Shirley's comedies," does not mention Confident Rapture in his one-page discussion of the play. He concentrates instead on the play's "noble tone," although he deplores the "incongruous melodrama," theatricality, and sensationalism of the piece. A. G. Swinburne, *Contemporaries of Shakespeare*, ed. Edmund Gosse and Thomas James Wise (London: William Heinemann, 1919), p. 297.

4. "According to Sir Henry Herbert . . . The Gamester is founded on a plot suggested by King Charles to the poet" (Forsythe, p. 357).

5. While *The Gamester* is usually referred to as a city comedy, it does not belong precisely in the same class as other such plays of his predecessors and contemporaries. The achievement of Jonson, Chapman, and Marston in the definitive English city comedy, *Eastward Ho!*, was an endorsement of middle-class values combined with satire of their limitations. Even more solidly bourgeois in its glorification of industry, honesty, and prudence is Thomas Dekker's *The Shoemaker's Holiday*. The city comedies of writers more critical of bourgeois aspirations reveal, as *Eastward Ho!* does, that their authors are to some extent patronizing "worthy citizens." There is outright satire in Francis Beaumont's *The Knight of the Burning Pestle*, a failure when first presented to a middle-class audience, but a success in its revival under aristocratic auspices in Shirley's time. Middleton and Massinger probe bourgeois values critically, too, in their city comedies, although the way of life presented there retains much of the attractiveness and even the charm of Dekker's busy, happy world. *The Gamester* may be distinguished from other city comedies by its greater attention to manner and

style, matters usually more closely associated with the nobility than with the middle class.

6. Prynne's alleged allusion (*Histriomastix* [1633], in an index entry) to Queen Henrietta Maria's appearance in a play at court "was the ground of his persecution" (Fleay, p. 406). Philip R. Rider notes that "Shirley was the leading dramatist of the Queen's company and had only recently been appointed Valet of the Chamber to the Queen; the phrase 'Servant to Her Majesty' appears for the first time on the title page of *The Bird in a Cage*" ("The Concurrent Printing of Shirley's *The Wittie Faire One* and *The Bird in a Cage*," *PBSA* 71 [1977]: 332). In fairness to Shirley it should be noted that he wrote the dedication before Prynne's sentence and punishment, which included mutilation.

7. *Don Lope de Cardona*. See Forsythe, pp. 190–99.

8. Marvin Morillo, "Shirley's 'Preferment' and the Court of Charles I," *SEL* 1 (1961): 101.

9. *Ibid*.

10. Sometimes attributed to John Fletcher in seventeenth-century printings, *The Coronation*, according to most modern scholars, belongs in Shirley's canon. It does not do him much credit.

Chapter Six

1. La Tourette Stockwell, *Dublin Theatres and Theater Customs (1637–1820)* (1938; rpt. New York and London: Benjamin Blom, 1968), p. 4.

2. Ibid., p. 5.

3. Albert Wertheim, "The Presentation of James Shirley's *St. Patrick for Ireland* at the First Irish Playhouse," *N&Q* 14 (1967): 213.

4. Ibid., p. 215.

5. C. V. Wedgwood, *Thomas Wentworth, First Earl of Strafford* (New York: Macmillan, 1962), p. 227.

6. According to Stockwell, the subplot in *The Doubtful Heir* is "based on contemporary Dublin life and represents the long-standing feud between the 'castle folk,' especially the army officers, and the Dublin tradespeople" (*Dublin Theatres*, p. 11).

7. *James Shirley, Dramatist*, p. 307.

8. Olaus is one of the many military figures characterized sympathetically in *The Young Admiral, The Example, The Gentleman of Venice, Honoria and Mammon, A Contention, The Opportunity, The Imposture, The Doubtful Heir,* and of course *The Politician,* too. Old soldier Olaus, a duke more at home with the army than at court, offends his King with straight talk; the Queen defends him, saying that he is "a Souldier, and not us'd to file / His language, blunt and rugged ways of speech / Becoming your profession" (III.i).

9. However, Bentley notes that *The Politician* "is one of the few Shirley plays for which we have no performance license under any title." *The Jacobean and Caroline Stage*, v. 5, 1138.

10. "The Sources of Shirley's *St. Patrick for Ireland*," *PMLA* 48 (1933): 811. Cf. Bentley, *The Jacobean and Caroline Stage*: "In the canon of Shirley's generally sophisticated plays, *St. Patrick for Ireland* is conspicuous for its crudeness; it is more like a Red Bull play than like Shirley's characteristic pieces for the Cockpit and Blackfriars" (v. 5, 1143).

11. It is difficult to see how the subplot could have been designed to attract the Irish citizenry (see n. 6, above), any more than the Globe prologue to win over the London audience.

Chapter Seven

1. These are the probable dates of departure and return according to Allan H. Stevenson, "Shirley's Dedications and the Date of His Return to England," *MLN* 61 (1946): 79–83.

2. When Shirley says, "A Poets art is to lead on your thought / Through subtle paths and workings of a plot" (*The Cardinal*, Prologue), he is referring to devices not unrelated to the concealment of the culprit in a mystery story or the twist at the end of an O. Henry tale—the "reversal" of expectations. In *The Politician*, where Gotharus is presented as scheming intriguer and Olaus as honest, open, plain-spoken soldier, Olaus outwits Gotharus by contriving the fourth-act "deaths" of Turgesius and Aquinas to thwart Gotharus's schemes; in the last act the "corpses" emerge alive and victorious. Such contrivances appear with increasing frequency in Shirley's later plays.

3. The characterization of soldiers elsewhere in *The Imposture* more than offsets Flaviano's cynicism. Volterino and Hortensio, colonels in the army of the conquering Duke of Ferrara, object to the cloistering of virgins, despise cowards, and mischievously get them drunk. They are always ready for bloody action; they are gruff where Flaviano is slick, good-natured where he is malicious. Essentially benign despite their calling, Volterino and Hortensio combine many of the traits of similar military characters in other plays. They receive more attention than such characters, except for the Captain in *The Doubtful Heir*.

Chapter Eight

1. Among these is a ball attended, according to Bornwell, by libertines of the kind associated with the Family of Love:

> Another game you have, which consumes more
> Your fame than purse; your revells in the night,
> Your meetings cal'd the Ball, to which appeare,
> As to the Court of Pleasure, all your gallants,

And Ladies thither bound by a Subpena
Of *Venus,* and small *Cupids* high displeasure,
Tis but the family of love translated
Into more costly sinne, there was a play on't,
And had the Poet not been brib'd to a modest
Expression of your Anticke gambolls in't,
Some darkes had been discovered, and the deeds too,
In time he may repent and make some blush,
To see the second part danc'd on the Stage;
My thoughts acquit you for dishonouring me
By any foule act, but the vertuous know,
Tis not enough to cleare our selves, but the
Suspitions of our shame. (I.i)

The play to which Bornwell refers is "Middleton's *The Family of Love* (published in 1608)," notes William C. Johnson, "The Family of Love in Stuart Literature: a chronology of name-crossed lovers," *Journal of Medieval and Renaissance Studies* 7 (1977): 103. "Among the dissenting groups particularly popular with early Stuart writers was the Family of Love. . . . detractors of the Puritans used the Family's name . . . to suggest the sexual promiscuity thought to be rampant among such groups" (p. 95).
2. George F. Sensabaugh says that "in Shirley's *The Lady of Pleasure* Celestina and Lord A. exemplify in many ways Platonic love in the court of Henrietta Maria. . . . Though Shirley probably had little sympathy for what he saw in the court and at times seemed to have his tongue in his cheek when he described the courtship of Lord A. and Celestina, as a dramatist he recognized that the contrast between Platonic love and open immorality would be extremely effective." "Platonic Love in Shirley's *The Lady of Pleasure,*" in *A Tribute to George Coffin Taylor,* ed. Arnold Williams (Chapel Hill: The University of North Carolina Press, 1952), pp. 171, 177.
3. He may not have killed himself: " '*Her.* I'd make you al some sports,—So, now we are even' could mean he's challenging Antonelli and the Cardinal's servants, and is killed after some sword-play. Gifford-Dyce added the stage-direction 'stabs himself.' " Frank Manley, "The Death of Hernando in Shirley's *The Cardinal,*" *N&Q* 12 (1965): 342–43.
4. Not all: among those who have dismissed *The Cardinal* as a worthy postscript to earlier seventeenth-century tragedy is Irving Ribner, *Jacobean Tragedy: The Quest for Moral Order* (New York: Barnes and Noble, 1962): "A play like Shirley's *The Cardinal,* although brilliantly constructed and no doubt extremely effective upon the stage, is merely the shallow imitation of only some external features of Webster's Italian tragedies" (p. 18). See also, for a general indictment of Shirley's tragedies, L. C. Knights, *Drama and Society in the Age of Jonson* (London: Chatto and Windus, 1957): Knights lists Shirley among those playwrights whose work shows "that

progressive narrowing of the scope of drama that leads from *Lear* to *Aureng-Zebe*" (p. 300).

Chapter Nine

1. Similarly, in *The Maid's Revenge*, a servant's earthiness contrasts with the noble sentiments of his mistress. When Castabella says of her brother's friend, "sure, he cannot be / Deare to you Brother, to whom I am not indebted, / At least for you," the servant Diego in an aside observes, "I have many deare friends too, my Taylor is one / To whom I am indebted" (II.iv).

Such wordplay, incidentally, frequently appears for its own sake and sometimes for mildly humorous characterization, as of the servant Whibble in *The Witty Fair One* when he is sent to fetch a horse: "If your Gelding be not ready in a minute, your Worship shall ride me" (possibly an aside) (I.i). Often enough, and at its best, Shirley's wordplay defines a state of mind, such as Aimwell's preoccupation with Violetta (in the same play), with whom marriage seems unlikely because her father has already chosen a husband for her: "Ile chuse my partner," Aimwell tells Worthy in response to an invitation to play cards. When Worthy agrees ("Make your owne election"), Aimwell wonders why he mocks him and in an aside says, "I shall betray my passion." Immediately following, Worthy says, "I find him," meaning that he knows, has found out, what Aimwell has been trying to hide. In a second aside Aimwell says, "You may, for I am lost" (*The Witty Fair One*, I.i). Such definition of state of mind through wordplay may seem simple enough, but its effectiveness in print or on stage is undeniable.

2. A popular image of the soldier may be inferred from the courtier Alamode's explanation of his preference for civilian life, addressed to the plain-spoken Captain Conquest:

> I am no tavern gull, that want protection,
> Whom you with oaths do mortify, and swear
> Into the payment of your ten pound surfeits;
> Upon whose credit you wear belt and feather,
> Top and top-gallant. Go to your Lindabrides
> I' the new brothel, she's a handsome leveret;
> If she deny free quarter, tear her trinkets,
> Make cullice of the matron; yet be friends
> Before the constable come in, and run
> O' the ticket for the dear disease. (*Honoria and Mammon*, I.ii)

Of course Alamode is as mistaken about Captain Conquest as Lady Lucina is about Captain Winfield in *The Ball*. Honoria honors Conquest and all soldiers for the protection they give society:

> A soldier merits first to be call'd man,
> By whom not only courts, but kingdoms flourish,

Unto whose several offices the world
Owes all the great and glorious names of honour. (II.iii)

3. The servant Georgio in *The Gentleman of Venice* considers the gentlemanly Giovanni (a gardener in civilian life) a "simple soldier," overly modest and naive, for refusing a reward for military service: "You know many soldiers / So modest, to refuse pay or preferment!" (IV.ii).

4. Shirley frequently draws on tried-and-true sources of stage humor. Lodwick in *The Grateful Servant*, pimping for an unsuspecting wife and urging a friend to seduce her, prompts a reference to the horns of a cuckold, still, apparently, in Shirley's time, certain to be greeted with raucous laughter.

5. While Shirley cannot be identified with late or contemporary Renaissance exponents of Baroque sensibility (among them Tourneur and Crashaw in England; Gongora, Marini, d'Urfé on the Continent), his more extravagant tragicomedies have their share of the sensuous macabre and the emotionally exquisite. Shirley may not be Baroque, but he can, on occasion, be bizarre. The public's taste for sensationalism may account for the melodramatic excesses in *The Duke's Mistress;* court-inspired cultivation of sentiment, for passionate effusions in *The Young Admiral*.

6. See R. V. Holdsworth, "Early References to Plays by Jonson, Shirley, and Others," *N&Q* 24 (1977): 208–209.

7. "In 1661 James Shirley's *Constant Maid*, first issued in 1640, was reissued as *Love will find out the Way* by 'T. B.'—this while the original author was still alive! An adaptation of Shirley's *The Traitor* was printed 1692. The original title was retained," but not the original author's name. Alfred Harbage, "Elizabethan-Restoration Palimpsest," *MLR* 35 (1940): 288.

8. Ibid., p. 289.

9. O. F. Morshead, ed., *The Diary of Samuel Pepys* (Selections) (New York: Harper and Row, 1960), p. 385.

10. Ibid., p. 417.

11. Helen McAfee, *Pepys on the Restoration Stage* (1916; rpt. New York: Benjamin Blom, 1964), p. 123.

12. Morshead, p. 449.

13. McAfee, p. 49.

14. See Chapter 5, n. 3.

15. *Selected Essays 1917–1932* (New York: Harcourt, Brace, 1932), pp. 161, 169, 170, 180.

16. *Themes and Conventions of Elizabethan Tragedy* (1935; rpt. Cambridge: University Press, 1966), pp. 264–67.

17. Ibid., p. 266.

18. *Selected Essays*, p. 247.

19. Virginia Ogden Birdsall, *Wild Civility: The English Comic Spirit on the Restoration Stage* (Bloomington and London: Indiana University Press, 1970), p. 4.

Selected Bibliography

PRIMARY SOURCES

1. Collections of Plays

The Dramatic Works and Poems of James Shirley. Ed. William Gifford and Alexander Dyce. 6 vols. 1833; rpt. New York: Russell and Russell, 1966.

Plays (The Witty Fair One, The Traitor, Hyde Park, The Lady of Pleasure, The Cardinal, The Triumph of Peace). Ed. Edmund Gosse. London: T. F. Unwin, 1888.

Six New Playes, Viz. The Brothers [1652], *[The] Sisters* [1652], *[The] Doubtfull Heir* [1652], *[The] Imposture* [1652], *[The] Cardinall* [1652], *[The] Court Secret* [1653]. London: Printed for Humphrey Robinson and Humphrey Moseley, 1653.

2. Individual Plays

CHAPMAN, GEORGE, and SHIRL[E]Y, JAMES. *The Ball*. London: Tho. Cotes, for Andrew Crooke and William Cooke, 1639.

————. *The Tragedie of Chabot Admirall of France*. London: Tho. Cotes, for Andrew Crooke and William Cooke, 1639.

FLETCHER, JOHN. *The Coronation*. London: Tho. Cotes, for Andrew Crooke and William Cooke, 1640.

SHIRLEY, JAMES. *The Bird in a Cage*. London: B. Alsop and T. Fawcet, for William Cooke, 1633.

————. *The Cardinal*. Ed. Charles R. Forker. Bloomington: Indiana University Press, 1964.

————. *Changes: Or, Love in a Maze*. London: G. P., for William Cooke, 1632.

————. *The Constant Maid*. London: J. Raworth, for R. Whitaker, 1640.

S[HIRLEY], J[AMES]. *A Contention for Honour and Riches*. London: E. A., for William Cooke, 1633.

————. *Cupid and Death*. Ed. B. A. Harris. In *A Book of Masques: In Honour of Allardyce Nicoll*. Ed. T. J. B. Spencer et al. London: Cambridge University Press, 1967, pp. 371-403.

SHIRL[E]Y, JAMES. *The Dukes Mistris*. London: John Norton, for Andrew Crooke, 1638.

SHIRL[E]Y, JAMES. *The Example*. London: John Norton, for Andrew Crooke and William Cooke, 1637.

SHIRL[E]Y, JAMES. *The Gamester*. London: John Norton, for Andrew Crooke and William Cooke, 1637.

SHIRLEY, JAMES. *The Gentleman of Venice*. London: Printed for Humphrey Moseley, 1655.

————. *The Gentleman of Venice*. Ed. Wilson F. Engel. In *Jacobean Drama Studies*. Salzburg: University of Salzburg, 1976.

————. *The Gratefull Servant*. London: B. A. and T. F., for John Grene, 1630.

SHIRL[E]Y, JAMES. *Hide Parke*. London: Tho. Cotes, for Andrew Crooke and William Cooke, 1637.

SHIRLEY, JAMES. *The Humourous Courtier*. London: T. C., for William Cooke, 1640.

————. *The Humourous Courtier*. Ed. Marvin Morillo. New York and London: Garland Publishing, Inc., 1979.

SHIRL[E]Y, JAMES. *The Lady of Pleasure*. London: Tho. Cotes, for Andrew Crooke and William Cooke, 1637.

SHIRLEY, JAMES. *Loves Crueltie*. London: Tho. Cotes, for Andrew Crooke, 1640.

————. *The Maides Revenge*. London: T. C., for William Cooke, 1639.

————. *The Opportunitie*. London: Thomas Cotes, for Andrew Crooke and Will. Cooke, 1640.

SHIRL[E]Y, JAMES. *A Pastorall Called the Arcadia*. London: I. D., for John Williams and F. Eglesfeild, 1640.

SHIRLEY, JAMES. *The Polititian*. London: Printed for Humphrey Moseley, 1655.

————. *The Royall Master*. London: T. Cotes, for John Crooke and Richard Seeger, 1638.

SHIRLEY, J[AMES]. *The Schoole of Complement* [*Love Tricks*]. London, 1631.

SHIRLEY, JAMES. *St. Patrick for Ireland. The first Part*. London: J. Raworth, for R. Whitaker, 1640.

————. *St. Patrick for Ireland*. Ed. John P. Turner, Jr. New York and London: Garland Publishing, Inc., 1979.

————. *The Traitor*. Ed. John Stewart Carter. Lincoln: University of Nebraska Press, 1965.

————. *The Traytor*. London: Printed for William Cooke, 1635.

————. *The Triumph of Peace*. London: John Norton, for William Cooke, 1633.

————. *The Triumph of Peace*. Ed. Clifford Leech. In *A Book of Masques: In Honour of Allardyce Nicoll*. Ed. T. J. B. Spencer et al. London: Cambridge University Press, 1967, pp. 275–313.

————. *The Wedding*. London: Printed for John Grout, 1629.

————. *The Wittie Faire One*. London: B. A. and T. F. for Wil. Cooke, 1633.

————. *A Critical Old-Spelling Edition of The Young Admiral by James Shirley* (1637). Ed. Kenneth J. Ericksen. New York and London: Garland Publishing, Inc., 1979.

SHIRL[E]Y, JAMES. *The Young Admirall*. London: Tho. Cotes, for Andrew Crooke and William Cooke, 1637.

3. Other Works

SHIRLEY, JAMES. *An Essay towards an universal and rational grammar.*
Ed. Jenkin T. Philipps. 1726; rpt. (facsimile) Menston, England: Scolar
Press, 1971.

————. *Narcissus, or, The Self-Lover.* London: Printed for Humphrey
Moseley, 1646.

————. *The Poems of James Shirley.* Ed. Ray Livingston Armstrong. Morningside Heights, N.Y.: King's Crown Press, 1941.

————. *Poems 1646 Together with Poems from the Rawlinson Manuscript.*
Menston, England: The Scolar Press, 1970.

————. Preface. *The Works of Beaumont and Fletcher* (1647). Ed. George
Darley. London: Routledge, Warde, and Routledge, 1840.

————. "A Prologue to the / ALCHIMIST / Acted (in *Ireland*)." In Vol. 9,
Ben Jonson. Ed. C. H. Herford et al. Oxford: Clarendon Press, 226.

SHIRLEY, JAM[ES]. *Via ad Latinam Linguam Complanata.* The Way made
plaine to the Latin tongue. London: Printed for Jo[hn] Stephenson,
1649.

SECONDARY SOURCES

1. General

BENTLEY, GERALD EADES. *The Jacobean and Caroline Stage.* 7 vols. Oxford:
Clarendon Press, 1941-68. The standard reference to Stuart theaters,
plays, and playwrights 1616–42 extends the listings and descriptions
in E. K. Chambers's *The Elizabethan Stage.*

————. *The Profession of Dramatist in Shakespeare's Time 1590–1642.*
Princeton: Princeton University Press, 1971. The working conditions
of professional dramatists include contracts with acting companies,
submission of manuscripts to censors, and collaboration in playwriting.

BIRDSALL, VIRGINIA OGDEN. *Wild Civility: The English Comic Spirit on the
Restoration Stage.* Bloomington and London: Indiana University Press,
1970. The realism and earthiness of Restoration comedy from Etherege
to Congreve have their roots in the English comic tradition and figure
as prominently as contemporary manners.

BOWERS, FREDSON T. *Elizabethan Revenge Tragedy, 1587–1642.* Princeton:
Princeton University Press, 1940. Elizabethan morality and earlier and
contemporary practice help determine the nature of revenge tragedy.

BRADBROOK, M.C. *Themes and Conventions of Elizabethan Tragedy.* 1935;
rpt. Cambridge University Press, 1966. Superior dramatic utterance
of Marlowe, Tourneur, Webster, and Middleton separates them from
the "decadents" (the latter including Shirley).

DEMARAY, JOHN G. *Milton and the Masque Tradition.* Cambridge, Mass.:
Harvard University Press, 1968. Interpretation of the texts of "Arcades"
and of *Comus* benefits from study of the contexts: contemporary work
in the genre and staging facilities on the sites available to Milton.

ELIOT, T.S. *Selected Essays 1917–1932*. New York: Harcourt, Brace and Company, 1932. Thirty-three critical essays on literary and related cultural subjects include twelve dealing with seventeenth-century English drama.

FRASER, RUSSELL. *The War Against Poetry*. Princeton: Princeton University Press, 1970. The war waged mainly by Puritans against poetry in sixteenth- and seventeenth-century England included many battles against the theater.

HARBAGE, ALFRED. *Cavalier Drama*. New York: Modern Language Association of America, 1936. The first of two parts deals with the influence of the Caroline court on the drama; the second surveys individual plays and playwrights from Caroline times through the Commonwealth period and into the early years of the Restoration.

HAVRAN, MARTIN J. *The Catholics in Caroline England*. Stanford: Stanford University Press, 1962. To judge even by the limited information about religious persecution available from the extant letters and records of English Catholics in Henrietta Maria's time, tolerance by the central government may not have been shared by individual communities.

HOY, CYRUS. "The Shares of Fletcher and his Collaborators in the Beaumont and Fletcher Canon." *Studies in Bibliography* 8 (1956): 129–46; 9 (1957): 143–62; 11 (1958): 85–106; 12 (1959): 91–116. Linguistic forms peculiar to Fletcher and to his collaborators (including Shirley) indicate the extent of each writer's contribution to individual plays.

KNIGHTS, L.C. *Drama and Society in the Age of Jonson*. London: Chatto and Windus, 1957. Half the book deals with the economic background of the period; the rest seeks to determine a relationship between the state of Jacobean society and the nature of the comedies written by Jonson, Dekker, Heywood, Middleton, and Massinger.

LAWRENCE, W. J. *Pre-Restoration Stage Studies*. 1927; rpt. New York: Benjamin Blom, Inc., 1967. Although each of the studies is complete in itself, the book as a whole works to relate dramaturgy to the physical conditions of the Elizabethan theater.

LEVIN, RICHARD. *The Multiple Plot in English Renaissance Drama*. Chicago and London: University of Chicago Press, 1971. The analysis of multiple-plot structures in over thirty plays draws most of its examples from Jacobean practice.

REYHER, PAUL. *Les Masques Anglais: Études sur les ballets et la vie de cour en Angleterre 1512–1640*. 1909; rpt. New York: Benjamin Blom, Inc., 1964. The greater attention to masque setting, costume, music, and dance (separate chapters on each) than to literary content (one chapter) reflects the emphasis of court (and court-influenced) dramatists themselves.

RIBNER, IRVING. *Jacobean Tragedy: The Quest for Moral Order*. New York: Barnes and Noble, 1962. Detailed studies of six Stuart dramatists (not including Shakespeare or Shirley, both of whom are dealt with only incidentally) explore the philosophical bases of Jacobean and Caroline tragedy.

SENSABAUGH, GEORGE. *The Tragic Muse of John Ford*. Stanford: Stanford University Press, 1944. The study of Ford's independently written plays emphasizes his anticipation of what have come to be called scientific determinism and unbridled individualism.

STOCKWELL, LA TOURETTE. *Dublin Theatres and Theatre Customs (1637–1820)*. 1938; rpt. New York and London: Benjamin Blom, Inc., 1968. The theaters in Dublin at first staged plays mainly for the Anglo-Irish, but eventually found more varied audiences.

SWINBURNE, A. G. *Contemporaries of Shakespeare,* ed. Edmund Gosse and Thomas James Wise. London: William Heinemann, 1919. Critical essays on plays by Marlowe, Chapman, Beaumont and Fletcher, Massinger, Day, Davenport, Nabbes, Brome, and Shirley find much to praise in the dramatists "rediscovered" by Lamb.

WAITH, EUGENE M. *Ideas of Greatness: Heroic Drama in England*. London: Routledge & Kegan Paul, 1971. Not limited chronologically, the study pays most attention, however, to concepts of the heroic in the English drama of the seventeenth century early and late.

WOOD, ANTHONY A. *Athenae Oxonienses* [1692], ed. Philip Bliss. 4 vols. Hildesheim: Georg Olms Verlagsbuchhandlung, 1969. Biographical sketches of distinguished Oxford graduates contain data unavailable elsewhere.

2. Shirley

BAS, GEORGES. "Thomas Zouch's Life of Walton and the Alleged Friendship Between James Shirley and Izaak Walton." *Notes and Queries* NS 24 (1977): 125–26. Walton's acknowledgment of friendship with English Catholics and his quotations from Shirley's works do not constitute evidence either of friendship with Shirley or of Shirley's Catholicism.

————. "Two Misrepresented Biographical Documents Concerning James Shirley." *Review of English Studies* NS 27 (1976): 303–10. One document deals with terminal dates for Shirley's alleged conversion to Catholicism and with the time of his departure from Hertfordshire for London; another leaves open the question of conversion.

BAUGH, ALBERT C. "Some New Facts About Shirley." *Modern Language Review* 17 (1922): 228–35. The new information clarifies the question of Shirley's status at St. Albans.

BENTLEY, GERALD EADES. "James Shirley and a Group of Unnoted Poems on the Wedding of Thomas Stanley." *Modern Language Quarterly* 2 (1939): 219–32. Association with Stanley in the mid-1640s is the basis for attributing to Shirley several poems commemorating Stanley's marriage.

BRAUNMULLER, A. R. " 'A Greater Wound': Corruption and Human Frailty in Chapman's 'Chabot, Admiral of France.' " *Modern Language Review*

70 (1975): 241–59. An interpretation of *Chabot* as a drama more of personal than of political conflict suggests incidentally that Shirley may have simply built on what Chapman had already written.

COGAN, NATHAN. "James Shirley's *The Example* (1634): Some Reconsiderations." *Studies in English Literature 1500–1900* 17 (1977): 317–31. The structural principles of *The Example* extend to *Hyde Park, The Lady of Pleasure, The Gamester, The Brothers,* and *The Witty Fair One,* especially in the integral contrast between main action and subplot.

CRAWLEY, DEREK. "The Effect of Shirley's Hand on Chapman's *The Tragedy of Chabot Admiral of France.*" *Studies in Philology* 63 (1966): 677–96. Scenes identifiable as Shirley's reveal his lack of understanding of Chapman's idea of stoicism.

FLEAY, F. G. "Annals of the Careers of James and Henry Shirley." *Anglia* 8 (1885): 405–14. Brief annotation of listed events in the lives of the two playwrights includes assumption of James Shirley's conversion.

FORSYTHE, ROBERT STANLEY. *The Relations of Shirley's Plays to the Elizabethan Drama.* 1914; rpt. New York: Benjamin Blom, Inc., 1965. A general survey of Stuart stage conditions, a short biography, and a study of the general characteristics of Shirley's plays precede lengthy discussions of sources, ascertained mainly by comparing parallel passages.

GREG, W. W. *"The Triumph of Peace:* A Bibliographer's Nightmare." *Library* 5th ser., 1 (1946–47): 113–26. The printing of the first edition was interrupted to include identification of the author as a member of Gray's Inn.

HOWARTH, R. G. "Shirley's *Cupid and Death.*" *Times Literary Supplement,* 15 November 1934, p. 795. Music for the masque may have been composed for only one of three performances, given at different times either as a private or a public entertainment.

KING, T. J. "Shirley's *Coronation* and *Love Will Find out the Way:* Erroneous Title-Pages." *Studies in Bibliography* 18 (1965): 265–69. The attribution of *The Coronation* to Fletcher is a publisher's doing; *Love,* attributed to "T. B.," is a revision of Shirley's *The Constant Maid.*

LAWLESS, DONALD S. "A Further Note on Shirley's Religion." *Notes and Queries* NS 24 (1977): 543. A couplet by Richard Brome in a commendatory verse is interpreted as an oblique reference to Shirley's Catholicism.

LEVIN, RICHARD. "The Triple Plot of *Hyde Park.*" *Modern Language Review* 62 (1967): 17-27. The three plots share a basic situation, treat each differently according to three traditional species of comedy, and in the process produce a unique dramatic structure.

McGRATH, JULIET. "James Shirley's Uses of Lanaguage." *Studies in English Literature 1500–1900* 6 (1966): 323–39. Shirley's distrust of language affects the quality of his characterization and of his thought.

MacMullan, Hugh. "The Sources of Shirley's *St. Patrick for Ireland*." *PMLA* 48 (1933): 806-14. The first of two parts deals with Shirley's indebtedness to biographies of the saint; the second, to contemporary English drama.

Manley, Frank. "The Death of Hernando in Shirley's *Cardinal*." *Notes and Queries* NS 12 (1965): 342–43. The death of Hernando may not have been suicidal.

Morillo, Marvin. "Shirley's 'Preferment' and the Court of Charles I." *Studies in English Literature 1500–1900*, 1 (Spring 1961): 101–17. Evidence from Shirley's plays and from contemporary documents suggests the reasons for the dramatist's decline in court favor after 1634.

Nason, Arthur Huntington. *James Shirley Dramatist*. 1915; rpt. New York: Benjamin Blom, Inc., 1967. The first of two parts is biographical; the second traces individual works chronologically.

Parlin, H. T. *A Study in Shirley's Comedies of London Life*. *Bulletin of the University of Texas*, No. 371, 1914. Shirley's city comedies share similar themes, structures, and tones.

Radtke, Stephen J. *James Shirley: His Catholic Philosophy of Life*. Washington, D.C.: The Catholic University of America, 1929. Five chapters deal respectively with 250 years of Shirley scholarship; the status of English Catholics in the Caroline period; biographical data; the religious sensibility revealed in Shirley's plays; and specific reference to Catholic doctrine in the plays.

Rider, Philip R. "The Concurrent Printing of Shirley's *The Wittie Faire One* and *The Bird in a Cage*." *Papers of the Bibliographical Society of America* 71 (1977): 328–33. Perhaps to capitalize on the publicity attendant on *The Bird in a Cage*, a new play, its publisher printed it at the same time as the older *The Wittie Faire One*.

Riemer, A.P. "A Source for Shirley's *The Traitor*." *Review of English Studies* NS 14 (1963): 380–83. The subplot is based on a 1595 English translation of Macchiavelli's *Le Istorie Fiorentina (The Florentine Historie)*.

Stadtfeld, Frieder. " 'Fortune,' 'providence' und 'manners' in James Shirleys *Hyde Park*." *Anglia* 93 (1975): 111–39. Usually praised mainly for its realism, *Hyde Park* deserves more attention to its formal treatment of social and theatrical conventions.

Stevenson, Allan H. "James Shirley and the Actors at the First Irish Theater." *Modern Philology* 40 (1942): 147–60. Some of the actors brought from London to Dublin in 1637 may be the same as those who joined Shirley in a new company on his return to London in 1640.

Wertheim, Albert. "Games and Courtship in James Shirley's *Hyde Park*." *Anglia* 90 (1972): 71–91. Interpretation of *Hyde Park* should take into account the park scenes in Acts III and IV as vital to the structure of the play as a whole.

―――. "The Presentation of James Shirley's *St. Patrick for Ireland* at the First Irish Playhouse." *Notes and Queries* NS 14 (1967): 212–15. After disappointing attendance at productions of London plays, Shirley wrote *St. Patrick* to attract Irish audiences to the Werburgh Street Playhouse.

Index